No Sex Please, \

GW01237189

Copyright by Spiros Doikas © 2013

Copyediting: William Berg

Cover art: Tim Wilson, Zontul Films Ltd

Typesetting: Elpida Chatzikonstanti

URL: www.sex-british.com

ISBN-10: 148264083X

ISBN-13: 978-1482640830

Spiros Doikas,
BA, MSc, KGB, Lav. Att.

No Sex Please, We're Brutish!

The exploits of a Greek student in Britain

CreateSpace Publications 2013

FIRST CLOWN: He that is mad, and sent to England.

HAMLET: Ay, marry; why was he sent to England?

FIRST CLOWN: Why, because he was mad; he shall recover his wits there; or, if he do not, 'tis no great matter there.

HAMLET: Why?

FIRST CLOWN: Twill not be seen in him there; there the men are as mad as he.

William Shakespeare, *Hamlet*

And as regards the therapeutic application of our knowledge, what would be the use of the most correct analysis of social neuroses, since no one possesses authority to impose such a therapy upon the group? But in spite of all these difficulties, we may expect that one day someone will venture to embark upon a pathology of cultural communities.

Sigmund Freud, *Civilization, Society and Religion*

One does not discover the absurd without being tempted to write a manual for happiness...

Albert Camus, *The myth of Sisyphus*

Contents

Acknowledgements

*I*t is, I feel, imperative that I, Spiros Doikas, BA, MSc, KGB, Lav. Att., pay homage to a great Martian scientist, Dr Paulus Silentiarius, who pioneered a very demanding path of research. Without his advanced insights into the nature of the natives I have strong doubts whether my modest study would have taken place at all.

Dr Silentiarius graduated in Social Anthropology (Single Horns) with a First Clash degree from Onanistan's renowned University of Loxford. Then he read for his MSc in Advanced Brutology at the University of Cowbridge, and ended up writing a PhD thesis entitled *Genetic Repercussions of Cross-breeding between Brutes and Humanoids* at the University of Central Petshire.

In his invaluable dual capacity as anthropologist and brutologist, he did the utmost to shed light on the intricate workings of the native psyche. The master's few surviving diaries were the main impetus for continuing his profound cogitations with my own humble thoughts.

No Emotions Please!

I am due to appear in court next week
Charged
with emotion.

—Roger McGough, *Vandal*

Englishwomen conceal their feelings until after they are married.
They show them then.

—Oscar Wilde, *A Woman of no Importance*

*U*pon arrival in Brutland I could read the big flashing signs:

WARNING: THIS IS AN EMOTION-FREE ZONE!

VISITORS FROM THE SUNWORLD ARE KINDLY REQUESTED TO ABANDON ANY EMOTIONAL LEFTOVERS FROM THEIR HOME COUNTRIES AND PROCEED IN AN ORDERLY FASHION THROUGH PASSPORT CONTROL BY FORMING A *QUEUE* SO AS TO AVOID ANY UNNECESSARY FLAGELLATION.

PEDERASTS, DYKES, QUEERS AND OTHER AFFECTIVE PREFERENCE MINORITIES WHO WILL ABIDE BY THE NO-EMOTION LAW ARE WELCOME. SPANKING, OR THE USE OF THE W.C. FOR THAT MATTER, IS AVAILABLE UPON REQUEST; HOWEVER, PLEASE NOTE THAT A CHARGE OF 20p WILL BE LEVIED.

SUNWORLDERS CAUGHT EMOTING ALL OVER THE PLACE WILL BE DEPORTED ***IMMEDIATELY.***

WARNING: THIS IS AN EMOTION-FREE ZONE!

And as I was staring in utter bewilderment at those phantasmagoria, out of the corner of my eye I caught sight of a British Airways Boeing 747 jumbo jet carrying three huge lettered ribbons that waved in the wind behind it:

*YOU ARE **KINDLY** REQUESTED*

TO

*ABANDON **ALL** EMOTION*

An Italian next to me was staring in awe, and asked his fellow traveller what this was all about. "*Lasciate ogni emozione voi ch' entrate*", came the reply, strongly echoing the words of the Florentine master. Which begs the question, if you abandon emotion, how far are you from abandoning hope?

De-Emotionalization Institutes

Do you know what "le vice anglais"—the English vice—really is? Not flagellation, not pederasty—whatever the French believe it to be: it's our refusal to admit our emotions. We think they demean us, I suppose.

—**Terence Rattigan**, *In Praise of Love*, (1973) Act II, p. 537

The English have no soul, they have the understatement instead.

—**George Mikes**, *How to be an Alien*, p. 24

This soul's prison we call England.

—**George Bernard Shaw**, *Heartbreak House* (Hector in Act III)

*O*discovered, however, that despite such admonitions there still remained—much to the chagrin of the people who believed in an ideal state—a considerable minority of the population who maintained some sort of an emotional, inner world. No matter how much they tried to dissimulate, emotion would emerge at the most inopportune times, obstructing the normal progress of affairs in Brutland. Ugly rumours had it that these individuals had been in possession of a soul—one of the most abhorrent miasmata that could infect a native.

It was obvious that these people were a disruption and a disgrace to the Equal Opportunities regime. They made heavy demands on national resources; complaining too much of an inner void, they became useless to society.

It was decided that measures should be taken: the state built specialized institutes in which cultural misfits would be gathered into large groups in order to undergo a de-emotionalization treatment. Those who successfully completed the programme would return to society, cured of their disease and in good working order. Those who failed were doomed to spend the rest of their lives in de-emotionalization institutes—under the best of health care, of course. In extreme cases, those who still maintained a soul would undergo a soul lobotomy or, if symptoms persisted, a soul castration/clitoridectomy (in accordance with the severity of each case and depending on the sex of the patient). Dr Silentiarius concurs and further elaborates on this issue:

> The natives use *clitoridectomy* as a cure for various conditions including epilepsy, catalepsy and mania, which are commonly attributed to masturbation, which so happens to plague this land. Dr Isaac Baker Brown, in his book *On the Curability of Certain Forms of Insanity, Epilepsy, Catalepsy, and Hysteria in Females*, gave a 70% success rate using this treatment. Personally, I have no reason to doubt

his claims, although, I must confess, my knowledge in all things medical is limited.

It was believed that in Brutland something like 20% of the National Health Service (NHS) funds were injected into de-emotionalization institutes. Even if this was true, the funds were clearly insufficient, as the streets (at least in urban areas) seemed to teem with emotionally challenged individuals.

A disease that commonly afflicted the natives and at times led to their being admitted to a de-emotionalization institute was the co-called Seasonal Affective Disorder (SAD). That disease was due to one of the fundamental characteristics of Brutland: clouds. Some people (undoubtedly belonging to the emotionally challenged population) had the audacity to demand the availability of that morally repugnant substance called Unobfuscated Solar Radiation. There was some talk in political circles of legalising it, but still it was a matter of principle for the Brutish democracy to avoid a potentially disastrous diminution of good old obfuscation.

However, I cannot help but express some doubts now about the so-called seasonal nature of the disease in question. I have strong reasons to believe that it has shown itself to be an epidemic of unimaginable proportions; I would suggest to the Health Committee a renaming of the condition as "Lifelong Affective Disorder" (LAD).

The One-Night Stand Phenomenon

The many faces of intimacy: the Victorians could experience it through correspondence, but not through cohabitation; contemporary men and women can experience it through fornication, but not through friendship.

—**Thomas Szasz,** "Social Relations", *The Second Sin,* 1973

The fact remains that England may be a copulating country but it is not an erotic country... Girls are being taken to bed, to be sure, but they are not courted; they are being made love to but they are not pursued. Women are quite willing to go to bed but they rarely flirt with men.

—**George Mikes,** *How to be a Brit,* p. 214

She is unable to sustain relationships and prizes her freedom above the collective good of the class. We encourage self-sufficiency, but your daughter [Britain] seems totally self-absorbed.

—**Lesley White,** "Riot Acts", *The Sunday Times Magazine,* 21 July 1996, p. 44

we awake to meet the day
we say goodmorning
and I wish you five hundred miles away.

—Roger McGough, *after the merrymaking, love?*

he most typical relationship between a male and a female in Brutland is called, in native terms, a *one-night stand* or an *(abnormally) prolonged one-night stand*. And this applies to every conceivable sort of relationship between the two sexes, including matrimony. The law says that others must be objectified and de-emotionalized in order to render a sexual relationship feasible. Emotion is the curse of the feeling classes (now long defunct in Brutland).

An anthropologist from Mars would observe that the natives have an inherent aversion to any form of touching that is not intercourse or violence. And, indeed, that is my observation as well. At times it occurs to me that if there were a way of having sex or procreating without touching, the inhabitants of Brutland would be the first to adopt it. It would strongly minimise any unnecessary risks of involvement and would further promote the paramount moral and philosophical doctrine of *keeping yourself to yourself*.

I am sure that with all of today's scientific breakthroughs, cybersex (including the currently popular varieties of IM sex, e.g., Skype sex, MSN sex, ICQ sex, IRC sex, and other forms of acronymic sex) will replace obsolete forms of intimacy; indeed, I consider the notion of "sex at a distance" ideal for the temperament of the natives. And perhaps one day, with the assistance of genetic engineering, Sir Thomas Browne's dream may become a reality for every afflicted native:

> I could be content that we might procreate like trees, without conjunction, or that there were any way to perpetuate the world without this trivial and vulgar way of coition.
> —**Sir Thomas Browne**, *Religio Medici*, pt. 2, sct. 9 *(1643)*.

However, some natives maintain that although coition is vulgar, masturbation is even more hideous, leaving the natives with few, if any, choices:

> FOR Fornication and Adultery itself, tho' heinous Sins, we have Frailty and Nature to plead; but SELF-POLLUTION is a Sin, not only against Nature, but a Sin, that perverts and extinguishes Nature, and he who is guilty of it, is labouring at the Destruction of his Kind, and in a manner strikes at the Creation itself.
>
> —**Anonymous**, *Onania; or, the Heinous Sin of Self-Pollution, and All its Frightful Consequences*, Thomas Crouch, London, 1723

Could this double restriction account for the high rates of violence in Brutland as the poor natives are left with no options when it comes to letting some steam off? And what does this entail for their self-respect? As Woody Allen says:

> Hey, don't knock masturbation. It's sex with someone I love!

❧

> You see, my darling girl, it isn't quite done over here to parade one's emotions so publicly. We as a race, on the whole, prefer to—*understate*. Do you understand my darling?—I was guilty of bad form, especially as, I think I did, I cried a bit when I told them... Oh damn the English! Sometimes I think that their bad form doesn't just lie in revealing their emotions, it's in having any at all.
> Do you like the English?
>
> —**Terence Rattigan**, The Collected Plays, Volume Four, *In Praise of Love, act I, p. 242*

Our cloudy climate and our chilly women.
—**Byron**, *Beppo*, stanza 48

According to my Martian colleague, Dr Silentiarius, certain patterns tend to repeat themselves in the way the male and female
of the species interact. For example, he found worthy of note
the fact that both sexes had managed to do away with phatic
communication, an achievement that even the most developed
intergalactic spiritual civilizations had failed to approximate.

He goes on to describe personal experiences that illustrate
this miraculous interactive breakthrough. I quote from his book,
Onanistan: An Anthropological Guide ("Onanistan" is the word for
"Brutland" in Martian):

> For the entire length of my experimental relationship
> I noticed a complete absence of the phatic three-word
> particle *how are you?* (and synonyms) when I was confabu-
> lating with my onanist mistress—be it a live encounter or
> a mere telephone conversation. This admired economy
> in superfluous discursive behaviour was, much to my sur-
> prise, matched by a further economy in extra-discursive
> communication, be it gesticulation, sudden changes in
> pitch, falsetto voice, meaningful nods, etc. The utmost
> achievement, however, was the way in which corporal
> interaction was restricted to the absolute essentials, thus
> avoiding time-consuming behaviour like hugging, kissing
> lightly, holding hands in public, and further demonstra-
> tions of "affectation" (affectation is the onanist equiva-
> lent of the Martian word "affection").

My experience is in accord with my Martian colleague's. An
addition to his observations would be the native euphemism
PDA (Public Display of Affectation) which is used in its abbrevi-
ated, acronymic form in order not to cause shock or embarrassment. A further linguistic observation on this term is the fact
that it is a *negative polarity item*, that is to say it is always used in a

negative linguistic context such as "I am *not* in favour of PDA—
how dare you, you pervert!".

Furthermore, an endemic sense of female machismo (according to Dr Silentiarius, the equivalent of the Martian "feminin-
ity") is based exactly on this aversion towards PDA. A female
that has developed a certain peer sex bonding would find it
insulting and swear she would never be caught *in flagrante delicto*
holding a male's hand. However, this does not imply that a similar feeling would arise if the scenario involved a mere "beast
with two backs".

> But even the English diet seems to me to give the intel-
> lect heavy feet—in fact, Englishwomen's feet...
> —**Friedrich Nietzsche**, "Why I am so clever", in *Ecce Homo*, p. 30

> What Englishwomen lack is the light-footed mobility of
> those Europeans...
> —*Vogue*, January 1997, p. 89

In order to enhance a sense of female machismo, indigenous
females have favoured the adoption of military boots and military marching techniques. Is this because they believe that it
makes them more attractive and leads them to a higher number of two-backed beast simulations than their non-boot-shod
and non-military-marching cognate females? Or is it some form
of female machismo?

I remember the very day, sometime during the first two weeks
of my five-year amorous sojourn in Brutland, when I was made
privy to one of the most arcane of their utterings. The time was
ripe for that major *epiphany*, my initiation into the sacred knowl-

edge—or should I say the *gnosis?*—of that all-important, quintessentially Brutish slang term, the word that endless hours of scholastic education by renowned mentors, plus years of scrupulous scrutiny into scrofulous texts, had *disappointingly* failed to impart to me, leaving me with that deep sense of emptiness begotten by *hemimathy*; the time was *finally* ripe for me to be transported by the velvety feel of the unvoiced palato-alveolar fricative, the *élan* of the unpronounceable and masochistically hedonistic front open-rounded vowel, and, last but not least, the (admittedly short) ejaculatory quality of the voiced velar stop: all three of them combined together to form that miraculous lexical item, the word *shag*.

I'd Rather have a British Man any day

What do women want? Asked Sigmund Freud all those years ago. According to Durex, they want a lot, but not a British male. The cheek of it. In an international league table the British male has been placed as the last choice for a lover by all our European neighbours. Ten thousand people in 15 countries were polled by Durex—and none longed to sleep with British men despite their long experience (average age of losing virginity is 16.7 years) and their reputation for safe sex (third best in the world).

It's enough to make you sympathise with the Euro-sceptics. The British have always had a great tradition of love. What's a few Casanovas and Julio Iglesiases next to the centuries-old tradition? There was Byron, who had everyone in the Regency period, including Lady Caroline Lamb and his own sister. Rochester, who makes today's writers of smut look like Enid Blyton (...) need I say more in defence of the British lover? (...)

The Durex survey found that the British were the most considerate lovers. Time for less Don Juan and more Fitzwilliam Darcy. This is what women want rather than Stud-u-Likes from the so-called sexual superpowers, the US and Russia. (...)

Who could ever fail to fall for the British modesty and understatement, the simplicity of approach ("You dancin'"?, "You askin'"?), the originality of thought (why have a boring candlelight dinner when you could take her to see Norwich City?) and the willingness to share Marks and Spencer jumpers. Paris, Milan and New York are passé and overdone when you consider the uncharted territories of Leicester train station, Surbirton shopping centre or Great Yarmouth pier (complete with funfair) for romantic encounters. And there's something very refreshing about the British male's complete lack of physical vanity—you may not love beer bellies but at least he's more interested in your body than showing off his.

British men are the best. And anyone who thinks Italians are the greatest lovers is in for a shock: a seduction school has just opened in Naples. Pupils pay 250 pounds for lessons in wooing. Before getting their diplomas, would-be romeos have to charm a beauty into bed.

Do you want to be seen with a man like that? I rest my case.

—**Glenda Cooper**, "I'd rather have a British man any day", *The Independent*, 21/5/1996

*T*o start with, I would like to cite the first axiom of statistics to which the data of all opinion polls are subjected: the axiom of full reversibility of results, which is in perfect accord with the idea that whatever is believed by the masses is always wrong.

British men are good lovers, alright. They don't flirt in a sly Casanova way, they are willing to share their Mark and Spencers jumpers with you, and they reveal their inner being, in understatement, with an eloquent gesture of ... vomit. To those of you belonging to the gloriously sought-after sex who are not fully cognizant of the particulars of this phenomenon, I would rush to sound my horn: be aware of the Englishman's *kiss of puke.*

British men are caring, committed. Right. The fact that one out of *two* marriages ends in divorce, the sheer number of single women having to raise children on their own because their husband has abandoned them—those are only small details that could not really affect much the Englishman's sovereign status as *simply the best.*

Well, why go to Paris, Venice, Vienna, etc.? Try Manchester canal for a romantic night and drink lots of beer (the drink of love) together: *By heck, chuck, it's wonderful!*

I insist. Manchester is an unspoilt paradise that has managed to preserve its beauty and magnificence throughout the centuries thanks to the natives keeping it a secret, refusing to turn their city into a commercialized mega-resort. Definitely the most romantic spot in the whole planetary system.

In Naples, it's all about sex—an overwhelming tradition of sex that is mirrored in the songs, the lifestyle, the chance sexual encounters with Neapolitan women (none of them would even think of marrying a Neapolitan man). It is said that the local media *deliberately* obfuscate the charms and graces of British men so as to prevent the whole female population of Naples from immigrating to Britain.

Ah, Neapolitan women, they *literally* don't know what they're missing.

Given the flirtatious and untrustworthy nature of Neapolitan men, it is difficult to explain why the population of the city hasn't died out yet. Some religious theorists have tried to refer this to *parthenogenesis*, that is to say, a divine infusion of miraculous fecundity into the indigenous female population, with results that mimic the more famous case of the Holy Mother.

It is a truth universally acknowledged that Byron was a great lover. He was such a great lover as to leave England and offer his services to the inhabitants of less favoured countries like Italy and Greece. Is it by any chance because he felt so forlorn with his own country's *"cloudy climate"* and *"chilly women"*? Let him speak for his patriotism here:

> I am sure my bones would not rest in an English grave, or my clay mix with the earth of that country. I believe the thought would drive me mad on my death-bed could I suppose that any of my friends would be base enough to

convey my carcass back to her soil. I would not even feed
her worms if I could help it.

—**Lord Byron**, Letter, 7/6/1819, to publisher John Murray

To return to the subject of the prowess of the English males, are
we sure that they are really such good lovers?

> It's especially good that, although British men are notori-
> ously lousy lovers, British women have learnt to expect lit-
> tle more and in fact find earnest male insistence (say, a ten
> hour Gallic span of attention to the clitoris) only theoreti-
> cally desirable.
>
> —**Nicholas Lezard**, "In Praise of British Women",
> *GQ*, 12/1996, p. 178

Well, I have to admit, opinions diverge:

> Englishmen are notorious lovers; it only takes the aver-
> age man ten years to ask the woman he loves for a kiss.
> Sometimes he proposes to a girl in maybe a year and a
> half—but not marriage.
>
> —**Peter Cagney**, *The Book of Wit and Humour*, 2596

And English women—are they so knowledgeable in the art of
seduction only in order to compensate for the lack of skills men
demonstrate in this department?

> And yet even in the dark years of this century, Britsex bub-
> bled under, though in an infantile way: ... an erotic vocabu-
> lary composed entirely of squeals and giggles; even the very
> words "slap and tickle", a euphemism for the carnal act no
> other nation on the planet could have coined... And that was
> all there was to it: we were ludicrously vague as to what
> the actual beast with the two backs was *about*. I mean what
> are you going to learn about sexuality when the only other
> phrase you have to describe it, apart from "s and t", is, "a bit
> of the other"? The other *what*? Leg? Bathroom? Day?
>
> —**Nicholas Lezard**, "In Praise of British Women", *GQ*, 12/1996, p. 174

But one should put the blame neither on men nor on women. Do you suppose you would be much better if you were brought up in Brutland yourself?

> Compared to your average Mediterranean male, we British are often condemned as unromantic—but then we don't have much to work with. While in France they have the *bistro*, we have the once-French and now very British-sounding *caff*. Frenchmen get to drink in sophisticated-sounding bars called *La Metro* (sic) or *Le Jardin*, while we drink in pubs with names like *The Bishop's Limpet* and the *Craggy Cock*.
>
> And then, of course, there's the food. Though we've imported most foreign dishes to spice up our cuisine, the main British meal is still fish and chips. They call it the great British invention, and indeed it's a king among meals. But the thought of spending an evening down at the chippy is not the kind of date of which dreams are made. It hardly competes with a candlelit Italian trattoria. Picture the scene: we seductively order a side portion of mushy peas, eye each other up over the pickled eggs, and I erotically pop a piece of battered cod into my mouth. As the grease oozes down my chin, I realise I should have taken her to the cinema instead.
>
> —*More!*, issue 220, 28/8-10/9/1996

And it's not just the food or the pubs. How is it possible to have romantic people in a country whose nights have been abandoned by the moon? *And, what about the stars?* Indeed, how can you have *people*, i.e., *humans?* Perhaps the etymology of the Greek word "anthropos" meaning "human" would support this argument. "Anthropos" is composed of the preposition άνω (up) and the verb θρώσκω (look). It is this romantic gesture, this romantic aspiration which is totally lacking in the natives' soul. How could it be possible to find moonstarers and stargazers in a country which is perennially covered by clouds and which has elevated such pointless exercises as *train-spotting, plane-spotting, tram-spotting* (and God knows what other – *spotting*) to favourite pastimes?

No Sex Please, We're Brutish

The British love sex—when other people are doing it. But we also hate sex—when we are doing it ourselves. What, asks, Henry Porter, does this say about our values?

—**Henry Porter**,"Too close for our comfort", *The Observer*, 13/10/1996

But according to Julia Cole... it is not the broad technical details that modern married couples lack so much as the artistry. A wag once commented that school sex education told you everything about the sexual act—except for the fact that you would very likely enjoy it.

—**Ross Clark**,"Not tonight, darling", *Daily Telegraph*, 10/8/1996

There was a time when failing to consummate a marriage was something to sing about: before the advent of the monasteries, which took celibates out of circulation, not doing it with your husband or wife was seen as a virtue.

—**Ross Clark**,"Not tonight, darling", *Daily Telegraph*, 10/8/1996

The British consider sex far too fleshy for comfort.
—**Henry Porter**, "Too close for our comfort", *The Observer*, 13/10/1996

As for sex, some Brits take a perverse delight in the idea that we are a nation of uptight neurotics.
—**Cosmo Landesman**, "May we have the pleasure?", The Guardian, 17/10/1998

The term Victorian has become synonymous with a certain code of ethics which was allegedly practiced during the 19th century, the time of Queen Victoria's reign. It seems that the natives have not yet recovered from the shock and are still suffering its consequences:

> In some bedrooms, it seems, the Victorian age lives on. There are still men like John Ruskin, who failed to consummate his marriage due to the shock, on his wedding night, of finding out that women had pubic hair; hitherto he had only seen smoothly sculpted, "naked" classical statues.
>
> —**Ross Clark**, "Not tonight, darling", *Daily Telegraph*, 10/8/1996

But it would be wrong to assert that Victorians simply saw the body as something inherently immoral; at the same time they saw it as something inherently divine and, as the truth lies somewhere in the middle, they suffered both ways:

> Others say they're both Christian and so didn't do it before they got married—and then cannot bear to do it after marriage. For them, sex has been built up into such a magnificence, with the Earth moving and the communion of the spirit that it can seem such a disappointment the first time they actually try it that they never finish and never try again.
>
> —**Ross Clark**, "Not tonight, darling", *Daily Telegraph*, 10/8/1996

Their parents, of course, did not help them resolve these rather unnatural ideas; on the contrary, they made things worse for them:

> The reasons for non-consummation are the same as ever, she reports, in spite of our apparent enlightenment on sexual matters. "Some fail to consummate because of parental prohibition: they think their parents would be against it. Some need to be told it's all right to do this

thing. Some married women have feelings that to submit
to men is wrong".

—**Ross Clark**, "Not tonight, darling", *Daily Telegraph*, 10/8/1996

Obese Queen Victoria (along with most other women of the
country) did not help, either, in engendering a feeling of healthy
sexuality in the natives; so, in desperation, they had to seek role
models elsewhere:

> Remember that for most of the last century this coun-
> try's iconic woman—our Madonna, as it were (in both
> the Catholic and the American senses)—was Queen
> Victoria. She might have been sex-on-a-stick for poor
> Prince Albert, and maybe that funny Scottish chap, but
> not for anyone else. For the rest of us, sex—unless prac-
> ticed furtively, hypocritically or illegally (or often, all
> three)—began on the other side of the Channel.
>
> —**Nicholas Lezard**, "In Praise of British Women", *GQ*, 12/1996, p. 174

But finding role models and not the thing in itself would not be
of much help. So they projected all their fantasies—and at times
their bodies—abroad:

> It is also, you will notice, foreign. We find it helpful to
> associate sexual products and practices with foreign-
> ers because—naturally—we could not possibly have
> invented them. (...)
>
> Abroad is where sex happens and where the British are
> most at risk. Sarah Ferguson is trapped having her toes
> sucked in France, Hugh Grant is caught negotiating with a
> prostitute in Los Angeles, and an MP is found in bed with
> another man on a continental holiday.
>
> —**Henry Porter**, "Too close for our comfort", *The Observer*, 13/10/1996

Oscar Wilde is right then when he sounds his horn regarding
unmarried men abroad:

> I don't think England should be represented abroad by an
> unmarried man... It might lead to complications.
>
> **—Oscar Wilde**, *A Woman of No Importance*

Sex indeed is foreign. And the way they talk about it seems to support this assertion. For example, the French are considered the main culprits: we have *French kiss*, *French letter*, and *French culture/sex/love*, meaning a kiss where you use your tongue, a condom, and fellatio respectively. We have *Greek culture/sex* which stands for the anal variation—although my experience tends to reinforce the fact that the Brits have far surpassed the Greeks in that respect. And as further proof of their exhaustive knowledge of the classics, *Roman culture/sex* stands for orgies. Last *and* least (by native standards) in the sex marathon come the Dutch: a *Dutch fuck* simply means lighting one cigarette from another. However, a degree of self-knowledge is portrayed in the fact that *English culture/sex/guidance* are umbrella terms for sadomasochist practices.

Despite the fact that they look down on loose "foreign" sexuality and appear to favour the ascetic, flagellatory variation, they would still do anything to "get their claws on them foreigners", clearly a sign of the Victorian hangover:

> Sure, we all knew what them continentals were like
> about sex. They were all at it from an early age, encour-
> aged, we didn't doubt, by their equally sex-mad parents.
> If only we could crack their continental cool and get our
> clammy claws on their tanned pert perfection.
>
> **—Brendan O'Connor**, "Slices of Exotica",
> *Irish Sunday Independent*, 22/6/1997

But why do they have to turn to foreigners for sex? Is it by any chance because the home-made product is rather uninterested and unavailable?

> These girls [local girls] were too sensible for sex. They
> wanted to play chasing and stuff. Courtship and sex were
> relegated to being a hidden agenda lurking beneath the
> endless games of chasing on summer nights
>
> —**Brendan O'Connor**, "Slices of Exotica",
> *Irish Sunday Independent*, 22/6/1997

This makes a marked difference from Victorian times, when
girls were apparently better looking and more willing, as can be
deduced from the serious novels of the time:

> At fifteen, appearances were mending; she [Catherine
> Morland] began to curl her hair and long for balls.
>
> —**Jane Austen**, *Northhanger Abbey*, Chapter 1

Unfortunately, modern Brutish girls have lost it, so foreign girls
have taken the lead:

> There was a "knowingness" about the way they walked
> that suggested the whole sex thing mightn't be totally
> alien to them.
>
> —**Brendan O'Connor**, "Slices of Exotica",
> *Irish Sunday Independent*, 22/6/1997

But still, regardless of whether they had sex abroad, or with
foreigners, and how much they enjoyed it, these highly spiritu-
alized creatures still see their bodies as an awkward *appendage
of flesh*. It is like being ashamed for having a physical existence;
or for that matter, for existing at all. The French have a way of
expressing the state of oneness and comfort with one's physical self, *être bien dans sa peau* (feeling well in your own skin). The
English counterpart of this psychological state is found in Joyce's
Mr Duffy, who "lived a short distance from his body" ("A Painful
Case", in *Dubliners*). Indeed, the totality of the indigenous population is afflicted by the "Mr Duffy Syndrome":

We are not a physically confident nation. When we think of ourselves making love we do not summon the blissful image of taut bodies coupling, but a vision of up-ended buttocks and too much cellulite. (...) Undressed we think of ourselves more naked than nude, the sort of nakedness you find in the self portrait of Stanley Spencer in which he shows himself crouching, pendulous, over his mistress' body and a leg of lamb. The common denominator of the three forms is flesh.

—**Henry Porter**, "Too close for our comfort", *The Observer*, 13/10/1996

And why is that so? Is it because of their non-prepossessing environment?

We are naturally a covered up nation, both mentally and physically. The ancient Greeks lived in Greece. We live in Scunthorpe, Edinburgh and Manchester.

—*The Independent,* 24/8/1996

Despite all this, how can they sometimes pretend that they don't really worry about it?

While the world's extremists are quite open about their fear of sex, the British pretend to be utterly at ease with it.

—**Henry Porter**, "Too close for our comfort", *The Observer,* 13/10/1996

Indeed, they are so much at ease with it that they have TV series bearing names like *Carnal Knowledge*, in which the contestants have to draw their favourite sexual positions and the commentator will tell them off with his rather camp mannerisms if he finds that the genitals are not saliently portrayed. *God's Gift* is another one of these gloriously at-ease series demonstrating the superior control the natives have over their instincts. In this one the contestants, among other things, have to demonstrate their prowess at toe sucking. It is no surprise, then, that some regions of the country where people are still healthy in mind would rather give such things a miss:

Yorkshire and the North-east are set to be sex-free regions, at least as far as independent television is concerned.
—**David Lister**, "Yorkshire becomes sex-free zone",
The Independent, 4/1/1997

Indeed, Yorkshire is a huge ecclesiastical community—much like the Vatican in Italy, although on a larger scale. Essex, on the other hand, and especially the *Essex girl*, has a reputation for extreme raunchiness. Why that is so I never understood, despite the natives' knowing grins when a girl states that she comes from Essex.

So, being a foreigner in this country, what do you do? How can you survive? How can you find wholesome emotional food? When it comes to surviving in a relationship, you have to know one thing above all: you must keep it impersonal. You also have to stomach the fact that one-night stands are bound to form a substantial part of your emotional diet—something like fish'n'chips. And if you die of emotional starvation somewhere along the way you'll know that at least you've tried.

The key to keeping your relationships impersonal is to follow the Brutish intimacy codes. Fasten your seat belts for the following revelation: Can you identify the ultimate criterion of superior achievement in erotic intimacy, the Albionic version of *Kama Sutra*?

Answer: Watching telly together.

I've always felt that English women had to be approached in a sisterly manner, rather than an erotic manner.
—**Anthony Burgess**, *Times*, London, 27/7/1988

Indeed, intimacy, even in sexual relationships, is not easily sustained. You might sleep with a girl but when they wake up they will ask permission for preparing a cup of tea and will insist upon thanking you for having had sex with them. Although sex comes so easily, hugging, especially in public, is something of a taboo: no self-respectful Brutish citizen would do that.

But perhaps nobody is more adept at the succinct expression of English post-coital embarrassment than Larkin:

> Nothing shows why
> At this unique distance from isolation
>
> It becomes still more difficult to find
> Words at once true and kind,
> Or not untrue and not unkind.

> —**Philip Larkin,** *Talking in Bed*

Or, if you never reach this dreadfully embarrassing situation and your sexual desires haven't been thoroughly negated or sublimated in the refined activities of boozing and fighting, you can still follow the advice of the local gentry, the Earl of Rochester in this case:

> Now wand'ring o'er this vile cunt-starving land
> I am content with what comes next to hand.

> —**Earl of Rochester,** *Sodom*

The Great
British Invention

What seems to me the most significant common traits in peaceful societies... are that they manifest enormous gusto for concrete physical pleasures—eating, drinking, sex, laughter—and that they make very little distinction between the ideal character of men and women, particularly that they have no ideal of brave aggressive masculinity.

—**Geoffrey Gorer**, in Gloria Steinem's essay
"The Myth of Masculine Mystique" (J.H. Pleck & J. Sawyer (ed),
Men and Masculinity, Prentice-Hall, INC., 1974, New Jersey, p. 138)

The English can be explained by their Anglo-Saxon heritage and the influence of Methodists. But I prefer to explain them in terms of tea, roast-beef and rain. A people is first what it eats, drinks and gets pelted with.

—**Pierre Daninos**, *Major Thomson and I*, (1957)
from the *Oxford Dictionary of Humorous quotations*, p. 109

Jeremy Paxman in his new book on the English argues that "for the majority of people, eating out is to consume fat-filled fast food, and to eat in, to be a victim of something pre-packaged".

—**Cosmo Landesman**, "May we have the pleasure?", *The Guardian*, 17/10/1998

Like most British people, I see my body as a disused Methodist chapel, now used for storage of unsold jumble.
—**David Stafford**,"Gut reactions", *The Guardian Weekend*, 5/10/1996, p. 14

As soon as the French start queuing up for baked beans, I shall commit harakiri, simply by leaning slowly on my favourite carving knife. Yes: the day the French start eating canned steak and kidney pie with a little tomato ketchup on top it will mark the end of a great civilization, the end of European supremacy and the suicide of a Continent.
—**George Mikes**, *How to be a Brit*, pp. 202-3

FISH'N'CHIPS—THE GREAT BRITISH INVENTION
—Seen in Leicester square, Big Ben city.

— "Could I have fish'n'chips please?"

— "No".

I stood there perplexed, with mind akimbo, as I could clearly see that the native equivalent of ambrosia existed there in abundance. Perhaps, five years before, I would immediately have caught her drift, but now it was a bit late for an update; I was already fully steeped in the mundane rigidity of Brutish matter-of-factness.

— "What do you mean, 'No'"?

I confronted her blank poker face. Ah, she almost cracked a smile. I was on again:

"Oh... right, you see I'm not used to a sense of humour in this context. I am not used to a sense of humour anyway".

She proceeded to give me the aforementioned traditional native delicacy. I was chuffed. I went to the cashier, paid the amount of one pound ninety-eight pence ("ta love"), and blissfully withdrew ("tarrah love") in order to devour silently the substance that was supposed to bestow immortality after a certain period of religious consumption. I could bless God for this meal.

That night, when I went to bed, I dreamt that somebody loved me.

The adoration of the substance *yeast* is indeed so great amongst the natives that they were not entirely satisfied with the mere production of its liquid extract. They had to come up with something more substantial, something edible, so that the two basic needs of human survival can both be satisfied in terms of yeast extract.

And indeed, they have invented *Marmite*. They use it as a spread for bread. This stuff is the closest you can get to yeast shit.

Yet, it is the closest you can get to edible shit—without mentioning that other famous affront to the human palate: *Branston Pickles*.

But culinary variety is not exhausted with fisn'n'chips and Marmite. What they apparently lack in sensual and sexual communicative skills they make up for with fine recipes. For example, they eat *spotted dicks* and drink *screaming orgasms*. And if these fail to satisfy, they go for something rougher—*blood pudding*.

A relevant extract from the Diaries of Dr Silentiarius:

> I find it quite relevant at this point to quote the long-deceased fellow-alien with the moustache and pipe who used to like *caviar* but who hated *generals*:
>
> *"Food and Intoxication.*—The natives are so greatly deceived because they are always *seeking* a deceiver: that is to say, a wine to stimulate their senses. If only they can have *that*, they are quite content with Marmite or beans on toast. Intoxication means more to them than nourishment—this is the bait they will always take! One cannot even offer them peace and plenty unless it includes the all-important pint (or even a can) and its mad-making power. But this mob taste, which *prefers intoxication to food...*"

He thought risotto was an Italian football player but he prepared this in five minutes.

—**TV advert**

I recollect with horror the first time I saw, smelled and tasted a dish called "moussaka" within the refectory context. It was an amorphous admixture of unsavoury ingredients in a highly liquid state. Other variants were *vegetable moussaka* and *moussaka with seafood*. Once, I saw it named *Italian moussaka* (!), and encountered for the first time the notion that this exotic dish might have its origins in the eponymous Mediterranean country.

But a query invaded my tortured mind and my stoical stomach: where did the pasta come from? That smooth, watery pasta I would be served that verged on being mashed potato? Was it, perchance, a product of that other exotic Mediterranean country—Greece? Perhaps I will never find the answer to this mushy question. It will have to be pigeonholed together with the other Big Questions like Existence, the Universe and the Many vs. the One.

There aren't many people in the world as meat-bound as the French. You can feast on falafel in Israel, sate yourself on salad in California, have hearty amounts of hummus in Greece. Even the red-blood devouring Italians can knock up a Napoletana sauce.

—"Always the English", *The Independent,* 6/11/1996

This is another instance in which ignorance about what is going on "overseas" is manifested. One should note, however, the writer's use of elegant variation ("can feast on...", "sate yourself on...", "have hearty amounts of...", "knock up a...") which makes one wonder whether here the elaborateness of style is a way of obscuring the uncertainty of content.

There is a widespread myth in England that "hummus" (crushed chick-pea and tahini dip) is a traditional Greek dish. Funnily enough, being Greek, I first heard about it (and tasted it) in England. "Hummus" is actually an Arab word and a Middle Eastern culinary invention.

> English cuisine is generally so threadbare that for years there has been a gentlemen's agreement in the civilized world to allow the Brits pre-eminence in the matter of tea—which, after all, comes down to little more than have ability to boil water.
>
> —**Fred Metclalf**, *Penguin Dictionary of Humorous Quotations*, p. 85

À *propos* of pasta. Within the Halls context, the cooking of pasta is commonly performed in the following way: first fill a pan with cold tap water. Then empty the pasta into it. And then put it on the fire so that it may boil. Serve hot and add ketchup.

Perhaps now I can support *a fortiori* the argument about "this mob taste, preferring intoxication to food..."

❧

> Food is about to be given an erotic makeover in a bid to make it sexy for the Nineties male, the man who thinks that beans on *brown* toast is *haute cuisine*.

> But can food really be sexy?... it is sunk deep into the national psyche that British men are not interested in cooking or eating.
>
> — "Could sex lure lads into the kitchen?", *The Observer*, 1/9/1996,

So, according to the above assertion, the following recipe is an example of such *haute cuisine*:

BAKED BEANS ON TOAST

Serves 1

Baked beans on toast is probably the most popular student dish. None the less it has much to commend it, being both filling and nutritious. A tasty variation is to add a few sultanas and 1/2 teaspoon (2.5ml) curry powder. On the subject of curry powder, beware of swapping recipes with friends who have hotter tastes than yourself. One of my friends nearly killed us with a curry she cooked. We found out later she got the recipe from an Indian student who likes his curries hot.

7-Oz (200-g) can baked, barbecue or curried beans
2 slices wholemeal toast

Toast the bread and at the same time warm the beans.
Vary by serving with grilled bacon or sliced tomatoes
on top or by covering the beans with grated cheese and
placing under the grill until the cheese melts.

—**Cas Clarke**, *Grub on a Grant*, p. 21

Why then this obsession with beans? Beans are for the English
what rice is for the Chinese. It's just that the English consume
their staple food exclusively from tins containing pre-cooked
beans in a tomato sauce with the *sine qua non* of E numbers.

I remember a group of university students who went to France
for their year out. What did they miss most of all things? Well,
it was packaged, sliced bread and, hey bingo... canned beans!
The availability of fresh French bread, croissants, remarkable
cheeses, fresh, local vegetables was not something that managed to impress them. And not just students. Even pop stars
give a good example when they go abroad. Speaking of which,
try guessing what Ringo Starr took with him when he went to
India with the Beatles... Two suitcases, one with clothes and the
other with Heinz Beans because he couldn't stand the Indian
vegetarian food!

You see, Beans at times are more difficult to find than drugs
and have to be smuggled into unwelcoming countries. Wars have
been fought in Brutland for who will be the beans mega-baron:

For discounters, offering the cheapest beans has become
a matter of marketing machismo... the trouble with
machismo is that people get hurt... Beans are convenient
and cheap wonder-food, offering a good dose of protein
and fibre. They also have a peculiar place in British hearts
and plates, popular in all ages, classes and regions.

—*The Times*, 5/10/1994, "Beanz meanz business"

As a rule they will refuse even to sample a foreign dish, they regard such things as garlic and olive oil with disgust, life is unliveable to them unless they have tea and puddings.

—**George Orwell**, "The English People", 1944
(repr. in *The Collected Essays, Journalism and Letters of George Orwell*, vol. 3,
ed. by Sonia Orwell & Ian Angus, 1968)

"My father will not allow foreign food in the house", was the plea of a flatmate, "it is only recently that he started opening up a bit, but still, I wouldn't go back home with a take-away meal from the Indian place down the road. It would be disrespectful towards him and I wouldn't like to do that". Well:

Stick to the rules, and you were eating ordinary, you were part of the tribe. Resist them and you were either a fool, a snob, a foreigner or Liz Earle.

—**David Stafford**, "Gut reactions", *The Guardian Weekend*,
5/10/1996, p. 17

The... conversation... was between two middle-aged ladies who had been out for lunch together. One said to the other: "I fell absolutely sick. That was a dreadful lunch we had in that restaurant". The friend replied: "Why did you eat it?" she was promptly told: "I had to eat it because I had paid for it".

—**Jan de Vries**, *Stress and Nervous Disorders*, p. 17

A friend of mine recounted for me the following story when I broached the subject of the rather peculiar mentality of the natives. He was with his girlfriend when she asked him whether he wanted to drink tea or coffee. "Whatever", he replied. She asked again, "whatever you make for yourself", he answered. "No", she insisted, "I asked what do *you* want". At this point he was at a loss. He had taken it for granted throughout his life that

he would have whatever other people had prepared and for the
first time he realised that he didn't really know what he preferred!

> This is the only country in the world where the food is
> more dangerous than sex.
>
> —**Jackie Mason**, *Daily Telegraph*, 17/2/1989

> There is no doubt, though, that faulty diet—an imbalance
> of nutrients, vitamins, trace elements and enzymes—
> plays a major role in any depressive illness... the first step
> I usually take in the treatment of depression is to change
> the diet of the sufferer.
>
> —**Jan de Vries**, *Stress and Nervous Disorders*, p. 45

And it looks as if bad cuisine and aggression go hand in hand (this,
as a way of further investigating the opening quotation of this chapter), according to recent research. You see, people in Brutland
were puzzled by the number of juvenile delinquents (some as
young as five!) who would joyride, vandalize, mug, burgle, and,
even *kill*. Now researchers maintain that the additives, colorants
and chemicals added into pre-cooked foods are the culprits.

It has been suggested that one way to remedy the situation would be to retrain the mothers in finishing-school fashion: "Mothers had to be taught how to cook. They simply don't
know what to do with fresh foods".

For more details, refer to the *Yorkshire Post* 14, October 1996:
"Cri-minally Bad Cuisine".

I decided to investigate in detail what my native flatmates were
eating. So, one night, when everybody was asleep, I ventured
out into the kitchen and into the cupboards in which they stored
the food. Here is a list of what I found:

Brand name	Description
Intrepid	spaghetti in tomato sauce
Tesco	value beans in tomato sauce
No Frills	eight hot dog sausages in brine
No Frills	beans and sausages in tomato sauce
Ye Olde Oak	eight premium hot dogs—sausages in brine
Sunpride	tuna flakes in brine
Westlers	four hamburgers—pork and bacon with onions and gravy
Westlers	beans and meatballs in tomato sauce
Um Glenbrook	bacon sizzle—bacon roll
Three Castles	pork luncheon meat
Golden Wonder	pot noodles
Heinz Big Soup	beef and bacon hot pot
Sweet Harvest	small potatoes in salted water
Sweet Harvest	mushy processed peas
Cambells	condensed double-cream of celery soup
Del Monte	peach halves
Sweet Harvest	pineapple chunks in own juice

I doubt whether English lads can be "lured into the kitchen" to repudiate their macho, canned/frozen/pre-processed diet: it is, you see, deeply ingrained in their psyche that an interest in tasty and healthy eating is a sign of effeminacy.

> Your diet probably consists of chips, pizza, chocolate and black coffee. You know you should be eating salad, but you just don't want to be a girl when it comes to food.
>
> —"Vitamins: Get Yourself a Dose!", FHM, December 1996, p. 291

1. Unstiffen your upper lip
2. Talk with your mouth full
3. Sit close together

—From a TV advert for spaghetti sauce: instructions on *How to eat Italian*.

"Dig in" (or "tuck in") are expressions that are seldom used, but monopolise their semantic vicinity in the thesaurus as the only native equivalent of *bon appétit!* Note that "good appetite" is clearly unidiomatic in English, having a definite foreign ring to it. Perhaps the absence of such an expression speaks volumes about the attitude of the natives towards food and towards eating in company.

ॐ

But why do these people have such a strange attitude towards food? Is it because enjoying it is just one more taboo, like enjoying sex? Is it because there has never been a tradition of good food? Is it because geographical and intellectual insularity has made this island inhospitable to foreign influences which could potentially civilize their palate? Is it because it just isn't macho to pay much attention to what one eats? Or is it because people cannot be bothered to prepare a decent meal, or just can't spare the time? To be sure, the above are not exhaustive:

> Stephen Mennel, in *All Manners Of Food* (Blackwell 1985), offers various explanations: that our Puritan heritage has left us ashamed of our appetite; that our monarchs have set us a bad example; that worship of all things rural has made us suspicious of anything urban and fancy.
>
> —**David Stafford**, "Gut reactions", *The Guardian Weekend,*
> 5/10/1996, p. 14

Though the passage of time makes the food no more palatable, most people soon become sufficiently inured to it. That was not exactly the case with me, despite the fact that I had experienced a regime of long subjection and protracted conditioning to it. (I have a rather peculiar resistance to suspect concoctions.) At best, one could say that I became sufficiently *manured* to it—*as if I were an infertile soil awaiting its scatological nutrients.*

And if there be any suggestion that I exaggerate, or any doubt regarding my impartiality, I quote the words of one who speaks with the authority of the native voice:

> It is time to put all thoughts of self-improvement behind us (...) To bring our rancid lard, our lumpy blancmanges, our etiolated salads, our radioactive fairy cakes, our fluffy Spangles out of the larder and put them on public show. To face the world as we truly are, always were and always will be. To proclaim proudly, defiantly, "We are British. We eat shit".
>
> —**David Stafford**, "Gut reactions", *The Guardian Weekend*, 5/10/1996,

As a final aside, I might comment that living in Brutland has been not only a unique culinary experience—titillating my taste buds with hitherto unknown tastes—but also an opportunity for great insight regarding the interpretation of certain pieces of world literature. For instance, had I been deprived of this opportunity I would not have been able to understand the hero of Kafka's short story, "A Hunger Artist", who, when asked to explain his fasting, insisted that he should not be admired. The reason he had gone on a fast was:

> Because I've never been able to find the kind of nourish-ment I like. If I had found it, believe me, I'd not have made this fuss but would have eaten my fill the same as you and everyone else.

Non Sequitur—By Any Chance?

England gives me the creeps. Life there is so dishonest, so unspontaneous. Don't you find it? I don't mean people are hypocrites. They are not—no more than anywhere else, and a lot less than in most places. But they're sort of dislocated from reality—and terribly repressed about everything. It's as if the whole country's missing out on life. And if I'm there for long I start feeling I am too.

—**Bryan Magee**, *Facing Death*, p. 77

It is a remarkable part of the British character which we happily acknowledge as our hypocrisy. But there is something deeper at work here. To call it hypocrisy would simply mean the public is pretending to virtues it doesn't possess. On the whole, I don't think the average Briton believes himself to be especially virtuous.

—*The Observer*, 13/10/1996

In this country it is enough for a man to have distinction and brains for every common tongue to wag against him. And what sort of lives do these people who pose as being moral lead themselves? We are in the native land of the hypocrite.

—**Oscar Wilde**, *The Picture of Dorian Gray*

he following is an event that happened during my studies. It has to do with a computer-related project. The person who was supposed to support us was absent for three consecutive weeks without any notice. I remember some rumours were circulating like, "Oh, I believe he is in France right now", and then again five minutes later a different person, "What are you on about? I saw him five minutes ago!".

Finally, one of the students brought this unexplained absenteeism to the attention of another member of the teaching staff who was higher up the academic ladder and—*hooray*, administrative hierarchy!—the absentee appeared in a lecture attended by computer project students, apologising for his behaviour and promising that he would turn up for the next session.

Indeed, he did turn up. He dealt with each student individually, discussing their specific projects or queries. It was a few minutes past the allotted teaching hour when he finally arrived at me. I explained what I was trying to do and he went on to give some relevant advice. At a certain point, when I sensed that his monologue was coming to an end, I asked:

— "So, is it true that you like John Lennon?"

— "Yes, but I am being paid here to teach you..."

And, obviously disappointed with my lack of a sense of duty, he departed in a sullen mood.

Non sequitur, by any chance?

When I caught a flatmate nicking my cheese *in flagrante* he went: "Nick told me I could have some but it's probably yours, is that alright?"

"Of course", I thought, "he said you could have some but it's probably mine, it makes perfect sense, you're not taking a course in advanced logic by any chance are you?". But I said nothing of the sort.

After such a display of subtle repartee what could I say?

"Have as much as you like".

Here is another example of forced logic which doesn't really make sense, apart from its obvious objective: to "prove" its point with any lame argument at hand. The following is an excerpt from a newspaper article which was chosen for the 1st Paper of the Institute of Linguists Diploma in Translation exam, November 1997, and it tries to support the idea of monarchy:

> The fact that we didn't choose a monarch doesn't make the system irrational any more than the fact that you don't choose your parent or child.

And I thought that gone are the fairy-tale times of Kings and Queens, which, admittedly, have a very interesting cosmetic value—for children, that is. Indeed, the above argument equates biological determinism with political arbitrariness. If we take it a bit further then we should not bother about choosing a political system, since we cannot choose our parent or child! To make the mechanism of the argument even clearer: All cats have four legs; my dog has four legs: therefore my dog is a cat.

Dr Silentiarius travelled in different areas of Brutland so that he could get the general picture—that means a rather big number of individual snapshots. He thought that this was the way to find the "truth"—if there was such a thing, of course. I quote a passage written during one of his trips in a place he calls *Paddyshire*, whose exact location eludes me. Perhaps this is because, according to Dr Silentiarius, Paddyshire is considered by Onanistan to be a decorative satellite state of no significance, only there for the occasional goods-exchange expedition. To be more precise, Onanistan had a sober carnal interest in Paddyshire's meat products, especially after the epidemic that required the hasty admittance of many Onanistan cows to de-emotionalization institutes. Those meat products, by general consensus of opinion, made "a most delicious, nourishing, and wholesome food, whether stewed, roasted, baked, or boiled". And, as if that were not already enough of a guarantee of quality, they were even believed to be equally good "in a fricassee or a ragout". For further information on these delicacies, consult Dean Swift's estimable tract, *A Modest Proposal*.

Talking of meat products, I find it imperative to include an advert for Hollands meat products (pies and puddings, mmmm yummy!) Now that I eat them, I realise that the fat man's words in the ad—"Tantalize your taste buds with my tasty treasures"—are just an understatement):

> Hollands believe that British beef is safe, however, following concerns expressed by consumers, a decision to import beef for many of our beef products has been taken. For costumers who still wish to support British beef, one product will remain unaltered. We will review the situation once consumer confidence on British beef has been re-established.

The magnanimity of the local meat companies has become proverbial. These people sacrifice their bread and butter so that the general public can enjoy their pig and cow. And all this, of course, without having been pressured by anybody. Well, British beef is good, it is British for God's sake, what more proof than that would one want?

ERASMUS ON ENGLAND

A climate at once agreeable and extremely healthy, and such a quantity of intellectual refinement and scholarship, not the usual pedantic and trivial kind either, but profound and learned...

[However, this was written in 1499]
—(As printed on the back cover of *A guide for Incoming Erasmus Students,*
University of Manchester, June 1994 edition)

Indeed, I admire that wonderful touch of honesty indicating the time when these words were written (perhaps they were valid then) thus pre-empting sarcasm on my part. I believe, however, that I will not be considered to be wildly free-associating if I quote the following excerpt, which appeals to me as an answer to the above with reference to modern day scholarly realities:

It was a perfect title in that it crystallized the article's niggling mindlessness, its funereal parade of yawn-enforcing facts, the pseudo-light it threw upon non-problems.

—**Kingsley Amis,** *Lucky Jim,* p. 14

Hanging on in quiet desperation is the English way

—**Pink Floyd**

"In the times before the yellow moon shone bright", the tribe suffered from a massive epidemic that was called *political correctness.* As the natives were very superstitious (even pantheistic at times), they believed that if they said "blackboard" then the blackboard would automatically feel discriminated against on the basis of its colour and consequently take offence.

What they did instead was to semantically bleach it and call it "board" instead, so that nobody would take offence. However, no historical records exist of blackboards demonstrating discomfort at being called "blackboards". (Some of them did complain, however, for a slightly different reason: some people would not write on them as they did with all other boards, but instead scratched on them using extra-white chalk.)

The disease of calling things names that didn't represent reality was exacerbated to such an extent that terminal cases, before giving up the ghost, would demonstrate symptoms of *nominal aphasia*.

The story goes that when once a native shouted "help!" he was ignored, since the receiver of the message interpreted this as "leave me alone!"

As a result of this, his help-shouting co-native was later found regurgitated by the waves...

> We have lingered by the chambers of the sea
> By sea-girls wreathed with sea-weed red and brown
> 'Till human voices wake us and we drown.
> —**T. S. Eliot**, *The Love Song of J. Alfred Prufrock*

But hypocrisy is not necessarily a vice. It can be a virtue; or should I say, it *is* a virtue:

> Yes, indeed. Without a little of the grease of hypocrisy, no system of representative democracy can function. This week's events add up to an exercise in necessary hypocrisy.
>
> —**Andrew Marr**, *A little hypocrisy is good for us all,*
> *The Independent*, 13/11/1996

When it comes to religion it is equally necessary:

> A partial lifting of the ban on investing in the drinks industry would enable the Church to "make a positive contribution" by entering into debate on issues within the industry... any investment in companies "wholly associated with alcohol" would remain under the ban.
>
> —*The Church of England Newspaper*, 29/11/1996

But of course the Bishop of Oxford would not allow this to
come out unsubstantiated:

> As a person who enjoys their drink, I have always felt it
> slightly illogical to have a ban on the breweries sector.
>
> —*ibid.*

And when it comes to sex-related matters, hypocrisy is even
more necessary than it is for politics or religion:

> "Porn's out, prawns in—W.H. Smith clears the top shelf
> to make way for tasty snacks". (...)
>
> The company will stock the magazines in 100 airport and
> station outlets but, more importantly, it will continue to
> distribute around 80 pornographic titles to the 26,000
> independent retailers that it supplies as a wholesaler.
>
> —*The Independent on Sunday,* 16/2/1997

But for the natives porn mags are not only a trademark of
sexuality but also a sign of a healthy sexual life; the top shelf
returns—reinforced:

> Anyone who thinks that the British are indifferent to sex
> should look at their local newsagent, and not just on the
> top shelf, either. British popular culture and the media
> are more saturated with sex-based images than ever.
> For example, last Wednesday's Sun featured 12 pairs of
> breasts and four pairs of male buttocks. No sex please,
> we're British, indeed.
>
> —**Cosmo Landesman,** "May we have the pleasure?",
> *The Guardian,* 17/10/1998

Indeed.

Fog in the Channel—Continent Cut Off

Two Englishmen went on a journey round the world on the same liner. They travelled separately and didn't know each other. Five months later as they were heading back across the Atlantic on the final stages of the trip they accidentally bumped into each other and although they had sat side by side on deck-chairs for months this was the first time they had spoken. The larger one who caused the collision said: "Sorry, old chap". The other one said: "That's all right. Nice day for the crossing, isn't it?"

—**Peter Cagney**, The Book of Wit and Humour, 2880

Between people who had just met, such a conversation could not have taken place in England.
"Is that a good thing do you think?" Mary asked
Terence said, "The English tell each other nothing".

—**Ian McEwan**, Psychopolis, from **Malcolm Bradbury** (ed),
Modern British Short Stories, p. 356

Doubtless insularity has bred in the Englishwoman an extreme response to Abroad: she may be terrified of flying and discover at age 32 that holidays in Norfolk are the answer to everything; or she may have a genius for the kind of ecstatic deracination that involves wearing a burnoose and learning dialects, accepting polygamy, submitting to ritual scarification, never coming home.

—*Vogue*, January 1997, p. 89

It is said that we are decadent, insular and lacking in national will. There is talk of "the British sickness".

—**Peter Grosvenor & James McMillan**, *The British Genius*, p. 534

The primary nature of every human being is to be open to life and love. Being guarded, armoured, distrustful and enclosed is second nature in our culture. It is the means we adopt to protect ourselves against being hurt, but when such attitudes become characterological, or structured in the personality, they constitute a more severe hurt and create a greater crippling that the one originally suffered.

—**Alexander Lowen**, *Bioenergetics*

There is safety in reserve, but no attraction. One cannot love a reserved person.

—**Jane Austen's** Frank Churchill (*Emma*, chapter 24)

> Oxford has no center. It's made up of dozens of colleges and departments, all doing their own thing; in the middle, where the center ought to be, there's an empty hole, a power vacuum. There's nowhere for change to start.
>
> Each college jealously guards its resources and autonomy. Academic standards also suffer as a result of this.
>
> —**Rosa Ehrenreich**, *A Garden of Paper Flowers*, p. 236

I was in one of the university libraries of Redbrick. I had asked for an issue of a periodical which was missing and they promised they would apply to the British Library in order to get a copy. The other day I went to one of the other major university libraries (a few hundred meters down the road) and I discovered all the issues of the very same periodical.

It is interesting that they preferred applying to a distant library, an expensive and time-consuming process, rather than check out whether the same document existed in one of the city's libraries. When I indicated the periodical's existence in the nearby campus they shrugged their shoulders saying: "Oh, we have nothing to do with them".

❧

> Yet the more insular we become—working from home, e-mailing rather than meeting—the more we rely on one central relationship.
>
> —**Lesley White**, "Riot Acts", *The Sunday Times Magazine*, 21/7/1996, p. 46

I had met my supervisor and we started a discussion about my dissertation.

— "You should arrange to see me sometime soon because I'll be off for two weeks from Wednesday".

— "OK", I said, "anytime that is convenient for you".

— "Well, I haven't got my book with me", he answered, placing his hands on his pockets and looking as if I had asked the most absurd thing in the world.

"Send me an e-mail", were his final words before he left the postgraduate computer lab.

His office was right outside—not more than 2 metres away.

In England there are sixty different religions, and only one sauce.

—Attributed to **Francesco Caraccioli** (1752–99),
Neapolitan naval commander

Elena, from Florence, spent some time in Halls of Residence as she was an Erasmus student in Redbrick. Of course, she had to share the flat with native girls. As a sign of hospitality she offered some mozzarella to an English flatmate, dropping a hint about the "limited" variety of native cheeses.

"Why?", the English girl retorted, "don't you like cheddar?"

After long research I believe that I've found the key to why the natives are so insular and so inhospitable. You see, it directly relates to their particular concept of happiness:

Few people can be happy unless they hate some other person, nation, or creed.

—**Bertrand Russell**

Silly old-fashioned me, I naively thought that it was the other way round; that is, "few people can be happy unless they *love* some other person, nation, or creed".

Had I not lived in Brutland myself I would never have come upon an extralexicographical meaning of the word "white". I had previously believed that it referred to people of Caucasian origin who possessed white skin—in other words, to the greater part of the indigenous European population. It came as a bit of a shock to me when one of my flatmates joyfully remarked:

> Hey, none of us is white in the house: I am Pakistani, Raj is Indian, John is Jamaican and you are Greek!
> [Names have been changed.]

Well, I would have shared his joy had two of them not been thoroughly Anglicized to the point of "not being able to live anywhere else" and the third suffering an identity crisis as he found himself in such an alien, but at the same time familiar, culture. I quickly forgot about the remark as something completely off the wall, an idiosyncrasy of my flatmate's idiolect, so to speak. However, I did visit a few ophthalmologists just to make sure my eyesight was all right. The matter was not completely resolved until three years later, when I was recounting my travails with indigenous criminals and indigenous police to an English friend of mine. The following clarifying conversation took place:

> —Well, you get a reasonably good service if you are white.
> —What do you mean "white", aren't I white?
> —I mean if you are not an immigrant.
> —I'm not an immigrant, I am a student!
> —Correction: *foreign* student.

That was the last day I double-checked on my skin colour—lest it was I who had got it wrong and the numerous ophthalmologists I had visited had been unable to diagnose this strange kind of colour-blindness. But it seems that "white" meant something far more that its chromatic qualities. Its meaning had been implicitly extended to mean WASP (White Anglo-Saxon Protestant), and that is why whoever did not fully comply with those requirements could not have been described as "white".

Months can pass without your meeting anyone who thinks he has anything Significant to Say. Silence is important here. (...) The English have internalized, and act quietly upon, ideas which other peoples feel they must express by noisy demonstration. The process is going on all around you if you live here. Sometimes you get startling signs of it, though it is not often visible.

—**Idries Shah**, *Darkest England*, p. 339

Here we have the beautiful British compromise: a man can say anything, he mustn't do anything; a man can listen to anything, but he mustn't be roused to do anything. By freedom of speech is meant freedom to talk *about*; speech is not saying-as-an-action.

—**Paul Goodman** *(1911–72)*, "Censorship and Pornography on the Stage?", lecture, pt. 2 (1959; published in *Creator Spirit Come*, 1977).

Another excerpt from professor Silentiarius' diary:

So what really matters in life, what is important?', I asked them. I was greeted with silence and indifference. "Aren't relationships the most important thing in life?" Why did I say that? I was so naive then, so innocently ignorant. They looked at me as if I were alien.

Well, aren't I?

Strictly speaking he was—but methinks they were alien themselves in a rather different way:

They [people who cannot express their feelings] give the impression of being different, alien beings, having come from an entirely different world, living in the midst of a society which is dominated by feelings.

—**Peter Sifneos**, *Affect, Emotional Conflict and Deficit: An Overview*

The typical Manchester iciness—nobody really speaks to each other and when they do it's on a really superficial, digging nature.

—**Morrissey** in John Robertson's *Morrissey In His Own Words*, p. 45

For three years in Redbrick I'd been going to the very same Yeast Extract Consumption Unit. There was this guy (or *bloke* as the natives say), more or less my age, dressed in a long black cape, tight, black leather trousers, a black T-shirt, and a tall black hat similar to those worn by the aristocracy of another era—or even similar to the hat Greek Orthodox priests wear. (However, he didn't have their long, white-bleached beard. In fact, he had no beard at all. Not even a goatee. And, against all odds, not even a five o'clock shadow.) To cut a long, complex description short: he was a *goth.*

Many a time we exchanged glances; many a time we consumed liquid yeast extract in close proximity to each other; many a time we danced on the same dancing floor. However, neither of us attempted any sort of communication—not a word, not the merest nod of acknowledgement.

Who knows, perhaps neither of us felt the need to do so. Indeed, why should we?

But insularity goes much further than just natural boundaries. For the native, a foreign country begins at the end of the street where he lives, and everything new is encountered with an attitude of mistrustful misanthropism. The *Ballad of an Elderly Man* by Sir Walter Raleigh (d. 1618) aptly expresses a kind of misanthropism peculiar to his nation (given that he was inevitably influenced in his judgements about the human race by the culture in which he grew up). This impression is reinforced by the particulars of the description, which allude to the defects in the

walking ability, the obnoxiousness of the talking faculty, and the
inherent snobbism of the English native:

> I wish I loved the human race
> I wish I loved its silly face
> I wish I liked the way it walks
> I wish I liked the way it talks
> And when I'm introduced to one
> I wish I thought what jolly fun!

Maybe this is the reason why even when...

> Crushed against his brother in the Tube the average
> Englishman pretends desperately that he is alone.

> —**Germaine Greer**, "Womanpower", in *The Female Eunuch*

Not unrelated to British insularity is the native concept of *privacy* which is very highly ranked indeed. I tried very hard to
understand why they would apotheosize this concept to the
detriment of other concepts like, say, *friendship*, and I thought
that perhaps the density of the population was to blame, or perhaps the weather, or the upbringing, or God knows what, until
I came across this:

> In the early part of this period [1860-1880] the new
> drive for sexual morality is concerned *not* with homosexuality but with "solitary vice". Pulpit denunciations in
> the 1860s are concerned with masturbation rather than
> homosexuality. The great theologian described the former as a new phenomenon, a new destructive vice introduced since the 1820s. The doctors also were concerned
> with its harmful effects and made special efforts to cure
> female masturbation, sometimes by drastic operations.
> *The public schools responded to this new threat by planning their schools so as to eliminate privacy.* Architecture
> and feeding arrangements were seen largely in terms of

whether they fostered or discouraged it. It was a special concern of the Church of England Purity Society (led by public school headmasters), which issued tracts against it aimed at the public and preparatory schools. [My emphasis]

—**Christie Davies**, *Permissive Britain*, p. 126-7

Self-Pollution is that unnatural Practice, by which Persons of either Sex may defile their own Bodies, without the Assistance of others, whilst yielding to filthy Imaginations, they endeavour to imitate and procure to themselves that Sensation, which God has ordered to attend the carnal Commerce of the two Sexes for the Continuance of our Species... Would all Masters of Schools have but a strict Eye over their Scholars, (amongst whom nothing is more common, than the Commission of this vile Sin, the Elder Boys teaching it the Younger) and give suitable Correction to the Offenders therein, and shame them before their School-fellows for it; I am persuaded it would deter them from the Practice, and by that means save them from Ruin.

—**Anonymous**, *Onania; or, the Heinous Sin of Self-Pollution, and All its Frightful Consequences*, Thomas Crouch, London, 1723

After I'd read this, things started making sense. A neural synapse directed me to Bentham's *Panopticon*, a mechanism devised for the surveillance of all sorts of inmates, which allows perfect visibility for the supervisor and absolute lack of privacy for the inmates. The main effect of the panopticon was (as Michel Foucault puts it in *Discipline and Punish*) to "induce in the inmate a state of permanent visibility that assures the automatic functioning of power". It goes without saying that visibility became a trap in the mind of the inmates, a notion that gradually infiltrated the collective unconscious of the nation. Indeed, the natives' obsessive need for privacy can be interpreted as the working of an unconscious panopticon complex carried over from Victorian times.

In the light of this epiphany I even managed to make sense of the state of mind which led to the making of such brilliant examples of native comedy as the episode *Divided We Stand* (1972) from the sitcom *Steptoe & Son*. In this episode, middle-aged Harold, who lives with his senile dad, decides, after the latter's insistence on repainting the house in dark green and chocolate, ("they don't show the dirt") that he needs "some privacy". To this end he devises a scheme whereby the house is effectively divided into two separate compartments. A turnstile is installed at the entrance and things seem to work somehow until they try to split the telly—the hottest object of desire (and dispute) in an English household even from the early 70's! What on earth will ever make them happy?

> The English ideal will be reached when everyone in
> England is living alone, on their own individual island.
>
> —**Antony Miall**, *Xenophobe's Guide to the English*

Thank you.
Thanks. Cheers. Ta.

On the Continent people have food; in England people have good table manners.

—George Mikes, *How to be an Alien*, p. 16

A 1975 report, for instance, reviewed several cases in which patients with certain lesions in the right area of the frontal lobes had a curious deficit: they were unable to understand the emotional message in people's tone of voice, though they were perfectly able to understand their words. A sarcastic "Thanks", a grateful "Thanks", and an angry "Thanks" all had the same neutral meaning for them. By contrast, a 1979 report spoke of patients with injuries in other parts of the right hemisphere who had a very different gap in their emotional perception. These patients were unable to express their own emotions through the tone of voice or by gesture.

—Daniel Goleman, *Emotional Intelligence*, p. 102

What follows is an analysis of key terms in the English politeness repertoire:

Sorry!—apologising is the best exercise in Applied Metaphysics. If you are good at apologising in Brutland you can get away with almost anything—even murder. So you shouldn't be surprised if somebody stabs you first and then wants to apologise and shake hands with you: it is only natural. And you shouldn't show any sign of consternation either—just act as if nothing had happened. Bear in mind that the utterance of this word sets up a primeval resonance made stronger by the fact that it is probable the third or fourth word an English baby learns (after "dada" and "mama")—only the word "ta" can challenge its primordial prestige.

Please and *thank you*—these are magical words. (An exhortation to a child: mind your *p*'s and *q*'s.) However, the way they are used is far from being magical; they have lost their inner strength, they are signifiers whose signified has gone hopelessly astray. The question: is it possible to say *thank you* with the tone one would normally use to say *piss off* or *I-couldn't-care-less*? And if so, what is prevalent semantically, the tone or the lexical content of the utterance?

How are you?—This is a *strictly phatic* three-word particle, simply a ritual exchange of words between people sharing a given space used to hide their embarrassment at meeting each other. Moreover, it's not meant to be used very often and it should by all means be avoided in any sort of conversation—be it on the phone or face to face—with people one does not know well.

I recollect a native woman recounting how she felt rather discontented with a colleague of hers because, when asked how she was, the colleague had made some grumpy remark about a problem at work. My friend justified her discontent over that reaction with the words: "You know, you're not meant to answer anything to that unless you're, well... dying".

Another researcher seems to have come to similar conclusions:

> I realised, agonizingly too late, that I had yet again said the wrong thing. In America. "How are you?" is a standard and meaningless pleasantry, exchanged with anyone one has met or corresponded with, often on the telephone as well as face to face. It was obvious from the chilly silence on the other end of the line that in England one does *not* say "How are you?" when speaking to strangers on the phone.
>
> —**Rosa Ehrenreich,** A *Garden of Paper Flowers,* p. 29

"Hey there! How are you?' and "You have a nice day now!" are the hallmarks of our national culture. I'm OK, you're OK. Let's all join hands for a moment here, folks.

Try saying "You have a real nice day now!" to an upper-class Oxford type. One can imagine the sneer of horror.

—*ibid.,* p. 192

Next Please!—Is always uttered with the robotic automatism of a worker turning screws in an assembly line. In extreme cases, even when working hours are over, some next-please utterers repeat this phrase to themselves and they derive some warmth and comfort from it; or, when they go back home, they ring the doorbell—to awaken the tenant.

The following is a description of a transaction which took place in an *off licence* establishment, otherwise known as an *offy.* It is quite hard for a foreigner to understand that this word simply means a place where you can purchase alcoholic drinks for consumption outside the premises. (The American equivalent is quite straightforward: *liquor store.* When I first heard the word offy, *offal* sprung to mind—which was somewhat *iffy.*)

Saleswoman: There you go, your cigarettes and your
matches and 67 pence change.
(She hands them over)
Client: *(counts the change carefully)* I think you've made a
mistake, you've given me £1.17 change, that's 50 p. extra.
Saleswoman: Oh, sorry about that!
*(Client hands back a pound coin, and fifteen pence in
smaller coins)*
Client: Sorry!
Saleswoman: It's alright, it's my fault.
(she returns the right change)
Client: Right, thank you very much!
Saleswoman: Cheers!
Client: Ta!
Saleswoman: Tarrah!

I wonder, where else in the world would somebody apologise
for undercharging you?

౭

The following, I believe, is a great example of native subtlety. (It
was my first experience with the "T" ritual.) A technician had
come to the house I was renting in order to fix the central heating:

"What comes after S?" he asked.

"T ?", I answered.

"Yes please,' he said.

It took me a while to realise that this was a way of asking for
a cup of tea.

So I went to the kitchen and put the kettle on.

When I returned with a steaming cup of tea he went: "Thanks,
thank you, cheers, ta, thank you very much", exhausting the
whole politeness repertoire within a few seconds. I felt it incumbent upon me to retort with an equally prolific string of pleasantries: "It's all right, you're welcome, no worries, it's nothing really".

To summarize, Brutish (im)politeness is not an easy phenomenon to define. It is inherently an endogenous fact, an indisputable state of heart, covered by the exogenous mask of a comprehensive formality repertoire which provides catch-words for every occasion—sadly enough, since a repertoire of corresponding emotional states which might generate polite behaviour are conspicuous by their absence. And this is proof of a higher impoliteness.

Pardon My French....

It was about a planet where the language kept turning into pure music, because the creatures there were so enchanted by sounds. Words became musical notes. Sentences became melodies. They were useless as conveyors of information, because nobody knew or cared what the meanings of words were anymore.

So leaders in government and commerce, in order to function, had to invent new and much uglier vocabularies and sentence structures all the time, which would resist being transmuted to music.

—**Kurt Vonnegut**, *Breakfast Of Champions*, p. 110

Neither do I think our English proper to express such violence of passion, which is very seldom felt amongst us.

—**Lady Mary Wortley Montagu**, letter to Alexander Pope [after translating a love poem from Turkish]

Some of us are naturally more attuned to the emotional mind's special symbolic modes: metaphor and simile, along with poetry, song and fable, are all cast in the language of the heart.

—**Daniel Goleman**, *Emotional Intelligence*, p. 54

The English have no respect for their language, and will not teach their children to speak it... It is impossible for an Englishman to open his mouth, without making some other Englishman despise him.

—**George Bernard Shaw**, *Pygmalion*

few comments by Dr Silentiarius on native speak:

On etymology. Their language is a mixture of Old Norse, Latin and Greek; however, they are very proud of its uniqueness to the extent of using the expression *it's all Greek (and Latin) to me*, when they want to indicate that something is difficult to understand. Very few schools, if any, continue to teach these defunct languages, and those that do have a reputation for cultivating affective preference minorities.

On phrasal verbs. The natives had developed a strong aversion to words that were reminiscent of poetry or music, as well as devices commonly used in literature like metaphors and similes; thus, they made a conscious effort to strip language of its strictly ornamental and jocose functions in order to make it a more efficient tool of communication.

One of the ways this has been accomplished is through the elimination of single-word verbs that were reputed to derive from old, barbaric civilizations, words like *compensate* and *tolerate*. Instead, phrasal verbs like *make up for* and *put up with* (respectively) took their place. Now, phrasal verbs (otherwise known as "two-word verbs", "verb-particle constructions", and "prepositional verbs"), were the outcome of the conjunction of proper verbs and neighbouring particles like prepositions and adverbs. Not only were they guilty of bestiality, but also of promiscuity, as a number of particles could combine with a proper verb in order to make a phrasal verb.

The paradox being that, notwithstanding the fact that some of their most sacred non-phrasal verbs had, unbeknownst to themselves, an etymology that harked back to those primitive and barbaric civilizations, they still frowned upon people who had been systematically abstaining from phrasal-verb usage.

In order to demonstrate the linguistic barbarity and
unscrupulous promiscuity of these constructions, I will
give you some extreme examples like *The cat crawled
back in under*, or, *Come on back up over* (!)

On shortening words. The use of words longer than three
syllables was considered by a great number of the natives
to be a transgression of etiquette, and the use thereof
indicated that the speaker was either extraterrestrial or
an Oxbridge graduate. Hence the word *secretary* became
secy, the word *husband* became *hubby*, the word *umbrella*
became *brolly*, the word *Andrew* became *Drew*, etc.

On the pronunciation of the natives. After careful observation and sociolinguistic analysis of the natives I have come
to the conclusion that their nation must be composed
of a number of different tribes—a conclusion based on
the local variations of pronunciation. For example the
vowel "u" (as in the word cup) can vary from /ʌ/ to /u/.
And is it rather amusing how each little tribe mocked and
leered at the pronunciation of the neighbouring tribe. For
those people, the sum total of their own little tribe was
the whole known world; nay, the whole known universe.
Everybody else was—rightly so—conceived as barbarian.
You see, they didn't have English as their mother tongue.

On RP. I would like to make a further observation on
what the natives call Received Pronunciation (RP). It
seems that people who managed to distort their tribal
accent into an RP accent (otherwise known as Oxonian
stutter) had the added advantage of creating a certain
type of reverbaratory field which had the effect of trap-
ping all the money within a ten mile radius. And this is
how the working classes were bereft of the greatest part
of their drinking allowance. The money which escapes
this field is called *pommies' pittance.*

On monosyllables. Allow me to quote a native: "Our
English tongue of all languages most swarmeth with the
single money of monosilables which are the onely scan-

dal of it. Bookes written in them and no other, seem like
shopkeepers boxes, that contain nothing else, save half-
pence, three-farthings and two pences".

—**Thomas Nashe**, *194, "Christ's Teares over Ierusalem", p. 2*

In order to enlighten people back home, Dr Silentiarius started
compiling a dictionary of some sociolinguistically idiosyncratic
terms and phrases, focusing on idiomatic usage. I quote a few of
them selectively:

> *Alright, [name]?*—This form is used as a standard saluta-
> tion when two people who don't use the phatic three-
> word particle meet. The addressee returns the same to
> the addresser, including of course the addresser's name.
> The names can be omitted in the shorter version.

> I remember a story told by a friend of mine from univer-
> sity. He was working in a nursing home and had two sick
> old men under his care. That night, he said, they would
> wake up every couple of hours repeating the same words
> with the only variation being the switch of the interrog-
> ative from:

> —*Alright, Brian?*
> —*Alright, John.*

> to:

> — *Alright, John?*
> — *Alright, Brian.*

However, the most notorious answer to this question can
be found in the world of arts. In the movie *The Full Monty*
two of the protagonists are stranded in the middle of a
canal, on top of a half-sunk car, after the girder they were
trying to use as a bridge had fallen into the water. Suddenly
they see a man coming who is taking his dog for a walk.

He says:

— Alright?

And the reply is:

— *Aye, not so bad.* (!!!)

And the man walks away.

In Kevin Kostner's *Robin Hood*, there is a gallows scene. Before the hanging a young man appears protesting about it and as a result he is arrested and joins the rest of them. An old man who is going to be hanged says to the hangman "leave him, he is too young". The hangman slaps him and proceeds with putting the rope around the young man's neck. At this point the old man says to the young one (both of whom are going to be hanged soon), "Are you alright?"

dodgy—if somebody is "dodgy" (unreliable, dangerous) then you should steer well clear of them. Similarly you can have a dodgy arm (injured or painful), be offered dodgy food at a restaurant (which will result in your having a stomach pumping) or be the owner of a dodgy stereo (faulty). The shades of meaning are numerous, and the regular use of this word will make you sound more native.

do (you) what?— (pronounced "jew what") A more colloquial equivalent of more acceptable expressions like "sorry?", "(I beg your) pardon?", used when you missed what the other person said or as an exclamation of surprise at what has been said.

fair enough!—This, like *right*, is another commonly used statement of acceptance. If you've not been initiated into the linguistic vagaries of this idiom, you may have the impression from its users that almost everything is fair. But I will not go any further in my analysis—*enough is enough.*

fuckin(g h)ell!— This is one of the most common exclamations of discontent. Be sure to use it as often as possible if you want to sound native.

Oh, that's nice—this phrase reminds me of a story I heard on telly about a posh woman and a non-posh one waiting in a gynaecologist's waiting room. After some irritable recounting of the expensive gifts the posh woman had received from her husband for the birth of each of her babies, the non-posh woman would always reply, "*Oh, that's nice*". At the end of the monologue, when asked what present her husband bought for her for their first baby, she retorted: "Well, he paid the fees for an elocution class so now I can say *that's nice* whilst before I would have said *up yours*".

Okey-dokey!— When I first encountered this form of address I was seriously embarrassed by my ignorance of native colloquialisms. The problem was that it sounded to me something like "hockey dockey" and the only connection in my mind was with that noble sport of hockey. I had visited the university gym and I wanted to go to the basketball court. So I asked the person in charge if I could do so. My ears heard him say "hockey dockey" and I paused for a moment, puzzled, before I exclaimed: "Well, sorry, it's not the hockey court I'm after; it's the basketball court". His reaction was to look at me as if I were an alien.

Finally I did find the basketball court; however, not without a lot of embarrassment, as, later, after asking a friend of mine, I discovered the real meaning of the expression, which is simply "OK".

right—this is a commonly overused statement of acceptance—or just a filler that reassures your interlocutor of your undiminished concentration. It is equivalent to *OK*, the way this is used by a nation called United States of Amercia (sic), which uses the same words in a different language and is renowned for its merciful feelings towards all other nations. To increase awareness of the natives regarding the overuse of this word, answer with the word *left* every time they say *right*. It is guaranteed to reduce its occurrence.

see you later—has a range of contextual usages that allows for numerous permutations of context. For example, when uttered in the morning after what was destined to be a one-night-stand. *See you later* should be tackled with a choice of different defamiliarising retorts like *see you earlier, see you previously* or just *when?* Of course, the natives might be disconcerted, since their expectations of mechanical and automated speech in interpersonal relationships are being thwarted; indeed, they might feel alienated for an instant. If you want to avoid that, just use the standard answering form of the native idiom—*see you (then)*.

sort out—we could argue that this entry is extra-lexico-graphical. It transcends by far the limits imposed upon the definition of a word in a contemporary dictionary. It seems that natives never cease to sort out something, and it has an all-inclusive frame of reference—from one's books to one's life. Of course, if phrasal verbs had a Royal Representative that would be it.

The Elgin marbles—Strange as it may sound, the "Elgin" marbles were not sculpted by Elgin—who was simply a proto-tourist with an idiosyncratic sense of property (Byron in his poem *The Curse of Minerva* is rather exaggerating when he states that "he basely stole what less barbarians won").

The English language is indeed crazy. A *public school* is not a *state school* but a *private school*, and a *grammar school* is not a school where one can learn *grammar*. Furthermore, a *school of fish* is not an educational establishment for fish.

English is the only language in the world in which you can drink your tea *and* eat it (not to mention the ability to have your cake and eat it)! And as if this were not enough, you can have *high tea* but there is no such thing as *low tea*. And then when you pay for your tea you can be *short-changed* but never *long-changed*.

How is it possible that the expression "cock up your beaver" (pardon my French!) means today something entirely different from what it meant to Robert Burns? And why do you excuse yourself for your French when in fact you mean to excuse yourself for your English? What would you say if you'd said something bad in French? *Pardon my English?*

Living Is Easy With Eyes Closed...

Nobody thinks about death, about his own death... because nobody lives a personal life... The cult of life, if it is truly profound and total, is also the cult of death, because the two are inseparable. A civilization that denies death ends by denying life.
—**Octavio Paz**, *The Labyrinth of Solitude*, Penguin. 1985 p. 46-53

Man's loneliness is but his fear of life.
—**Eugene O'Neill** (1888–1953), Lazarus, in *Lazarus Laughed*, act III, sc. ii.

At your age I looked for hardship, danger, horror, and death, that I might feel the life in me more intensely. I did not let the fear of death govern my life; and my reward was, I had my life.
—**George Bernard Shaw**, *Heartbreak House*, Act II

I'd been clutching the empty bottle like grim death, I remember, as if I were holding on to life, in a way.
—**Kingsley Amis**, *Lucky Jim*, p. 18

Perhaps it is only those who understand just how fragile life is who know how precious it is. Once when I was taking part in a conference in Britain, the participants were interviewed by the BBC. At the same time they talked to a woman who was actually dying. She was so distraught with fear, because she had not really thought that death was real. Now she knew. She had just one message to those who would survive her: to take life, and death, seriously.

—**Sogyal Rinpoche,** *The Tibetan Book of Living and Dying*, p. 23

One can live for years sometimes without living at all, and then all life comes crowding into one single hour.

—**Oscar Wilde,** *Vera, or The Nihilists*

People in Brutland are born and die without the luminous interval in-between. The dreamcrossed twilight between the womb and tomb manages somehow to escape them. Why is that? Well, for a start, the sun in this neck of the woods is obscured by the clouds. But there is another, much deeper reason. People in Brutland are led to believe that they will exist forever (a common psychological quirk of the tribe); they can therefore afford the luxury of infinitely postponing *life*.

Life and its derivatives, in Brutish, are taboo words. People are scared to live because they are afraid of *death*.

Hmm... *death*. That's another taboo word. Not as strong though.

Indeed, death has no dominion in this latitude. It has been exiled, together with the aged of the species, to the "scenic" coastal cities. Cities exclusively reserved as a place where one can make one's quietus through graceful degradation, quietly and discreetly.

However, the existence of death still remains a sibylline notion. Nobody really knows for sure if it exists or not as nobody has ever seen anybody dying.

Perhaps death is just fiction.

As life is.

> "Mr Stevens, I'm very sorry. Your father passed away about four minutes ago".
> "I see".
> (...)
> "Will you come up and see him?"
> "I'm very busy just now, Miss Kenton. In a little while perhaps".
> "In that case Mr. Stevens, will you permit me to close his eyes?"
> "I would be most grateful if you would, Miss Kenton".
> She began to climb the staircase, but I stopped her, saying: "Miss Kenton, please don't think me unduly improper in not ascending to see my father in his deceased condition just at this moment. You see, I know my father would have wished me to carry on just now".
> —**Kazuo Ishiguro**,*The Remains of The Day*, p. 106

Gentlemen. It is a truth universally acknowledged that an old woman in possession of a good fortune must be in want of a rest house. *Granny farming* is one of the most profitable national industries that demand, by the sheer fact of their unlimited potential and record-breaking productivity, the financial and moral support of the state.

One ought to ignore the demagogic understatements of the political opposition, those unscrupulous self-appointed moral watchdogs, dismissing one of our greatest national industries. These are voices that undermine all that is sacred and worthy of respect. Do you recollect what the spokesman of the opposition had to say the other day? "They do yield a fairly decent crop—better than potatoes I dare say!" I think that's complete and utter poppycock—do I not meet with your accord on this?

If we, the people of Brutland, fail to give our wholehearted support to this admired infrastructure, what will become of the moral fabric of the nation? Granny farms, with their superior manure and endless reserves of ripe cadavers, fertilize the very soul of the nation. The message to the self-appointed moral watchdogs of our nanny state is clear and simple: "Time, *ladies*, please".

Some people who were not content with the lifelessness of life invented another "life", a life after the end of lifelessness, what they called a *life after death*. It was meant to be a glorious thing, the best thing that could ever happen to you, but, paradoxically, those *especially* who truly believed in it seemed *utterly* terrified when time to shuffle off their mortal coil was drawing nigh.

They didn't know though why they had to come up with this ingenuous *fictum*, they didn't know that they did it because they had, unbeknownst to themselves, wasted their lives by living them; they didn't know that *it is not death that truly terrifies but the inability to live.*

The Metaphysics of Real Ale Consumption

A dreamy smile stretched his face in the darkness as he savoured again in retrospect that wonderful moment at ten o'clock. It had been like a first authentic experience of art, of human goodness, a stern, rapt, almost devotional exaltation. Gulping down what he'd assumed must be his last pint of the evening, he'd noticed that drinks were still being ordered and served, that people were still coming in and that their expressions were confident, not anxious, that a new sixpence had tinkled into the works of the bar-billiard table. Illumination had come when the white-coated barman struggled in with 2 fresh crates of Guinness. (...) His gratitude had been inexpressible in words; only further calls at the bar could pay that happy debt. As a result he'd spent more than he could afford and drunk more than he ought, and yet he felt nothing but satisfaction and peace.

—**Kingsley Amis**, *Lucky Jim*, p. 54

Open any English newspaper and you will find complaints about pubs: of poor service, weak beer, horrifying snacks and total boredom. One wonders why people use such places at all. Perhaps because they have been told that suffering is good for the soul.

—**Idries Shah**, *Darkest England*, p. 294

To finer nostrils, this English taint of spleen and alcoholic excess, for which, owing to good reasons, it is used as an antidote—the finer poison to neutralize the coarser: a finer form of poisoning is in fact a step towards spiritualization. The English coarseness and rustic demureness is still most satisfactorily disguised by Christian pantomime, and by praying and psalm-singing (or, more correctly, it is thereby explained and differently expressed); and for the herd of drunkards and rakes who formerly learned moral grunting under the influence of Methodism...

They are not a philosophical race—the English.... Schelling *rightly* said, "*Je méprise Locke*"; in the struggle against the English mechanical stultification of the world... It is characteristic of such an unphilosophical race to hold on firmly to Christianity—they *need* its discipline for "moralising" and humanising. The Englishman, more gloomy, sensual, headstrong, and brutal than the German—is for that very reason, as the baser of the two, also the most pious: he has all the *more need* of Christianity.

—**Friedrich Nietzsche**, *Beyond Good and Evil*, p. 252

What a pity it is that we have no amusements in England but vice and religion!

—**Sydney Smith** (1771–1845), English clergyman, writer. Quoted in: Hesketh Pearson, *The Smith of Smiths*, ch. 10 (1934).

Sir William Harcourt argued that "as much of the history
of England had been brought about in public houses as in
the House of Commons".

—**Brian Harrison**, *Drink and the Victorians*, p. 45

If there was a God in Brutland, which abode would He or She
favour? I swear that He or She would be bound to be the sovereign ruler of a Yeast Extract Consumption Unit—what the
natives call *publican*. Or, alternatively, He or She would merely
inhabit it and demand from His or Her congregation the performance of proper rites of worship (including Holy Communion)
only within the premises of that hallowed edifice:

Why can't we drink when we like?

It IS a great British failing that we invariably make mock-
eries of our national institutions.

Even before the Church of England considered it a fit
topic for debate whether or not priests should believe in
God, a latter-day idol Eric Idle to be precise had already
laid into the one place most of us genuinely feel at home
on Sundays: the pub.

—*The Times*, 2 August 1994, "No bar to pub opening", **Peter Millar**.

Something that leads me to the conclusion that Beer, Religion,
Pubs, National Pride, Alcoholics Anonymous and *joie de vivre* are
concepts synonymous:

British beer is today widely acknowledged to be a subject
for pride, as subtle, varied and demanding on the educated palate as the products of Burgundy micro-climates.
But one crucial difference is that our ales are at their best
only when pulled by handpump from a barrel properly
racked in a well-run cellar. In short, good beer and good
pubs are synonymous.

—*ibid.*

And, to recapitulate, I should like to emphasize that God can only be properly worshipped within the sanctified space of Brutland's state-of-the-fart Yeast Extract Consumption Unit.

Indeed, a recent decrease of these establishments can only bring on degeneration and possession of the people's angelic spirit by those subservient to the Prince of Devils. Those venues that prop up religious institutions and strengthen the nation's moral fabric should by all conceivable means be further sustained and empowered. It is absurd and blasphemous to house the *soi-disant* homeless in the holy niches of God:

> Trade figures estimate there are about 65,000 left, but it would take a blind, and insensitive, optimist not to realise that *we are in danger of being cavalier about the erosion of an essential part of the English way of life.* Look at the fate of any village where the public house has been bought up, closed down and converted into accommodation: *strand of community life dies with it.* [My emphasis]
>
> —*ibid.*

2&

> The bonds between drink and every aspect of life in a predominantly agricultural society had hitherto made teetotalers as rare as atheists. Indeed, in the early Victorian period, religion and drink were often abandoned together by the same individuals...
>
> —**Brian Harrison**, *Drink and the Victorians*, p. 44

> By drinking deeply one asserted one's virility; working men marked their sons' maturity by making them publicly drink at a "rearing".
>
> —*ibid., p. 39*

It is one of the most adhered-to, unwritten laws of Brutland that whoever doth enter the temple of God is under the severe moral obligation of consuming at least a whole *pint* of yeast extract. Individuals that do otherwise, either by means of consuming in *half-a-pint* units or by means of consuming uncustomary types of yeast extract are frequently frowned upon and secretly excommunicated. For example, *snakebite* (beer and cider) drinkers are brimming with the right hormones, whereas *shandy* (lager and Sprite) drinkers are bound to be rather deficient in the virility department.

It is due to native ingenuity that a method has been devised by which one may distinguish between the former and the latter (the so-called *poofs*). Being able to further differentiate between the two aforementioned species is a matter of great importance, as it may prove tricky when one is found in the fuzzy condition of rapture that consumption of the sacrament often leads to.

To clear things up a little: religious ecstasy is bound to lead to *empathogenesis*, a condition involving an increase in spontaneity and communicative ability; one should be very cautious lest he or she empathise with an individual that has the inappropriate twenty-fourth chromosome. Therefore, a male would not be able to discern between a female and a poof on the sole basis of the consumption of yeast extract in *half-a-pint* units (of which both are capable), and a further clue becomes urgently needed.

However, those with increased serotonin levels, induced by the intervention of the Holy Dove, wouldn't really give a toss.

In settling an island, the first building erected by a Spaniard will be a church; by a Frenchman a fort; by a Dutchman, a warehouse; and by a Englishman, an alehouse.

—**G.L Aperson**, *English Proverbs and proverbial phrases*

There were a few empty rooms in the house where I was living, so the landlord wanted to fill them up. But it was I who was going to do all the showing around. Presently, a couple of first year English males came round, and after they'd had a thorough look around the house whilst I was describing it to them, as we went to the kitchen for a cup of tea, the burning question, the all-important piece of factual knowledge that would make the real difference and resolve all existential angst, finally found its expression in the form of the interrogatory: "How far is the nearest pub?".

Why do some Brits go abroad to drink like fish and fight for fun? "I think that's just a nasty hangover from the jingoism and imperial chauvinism of our past", says Dr Helen Haste, head of Psychology at the University of Bath.

—**Cosmo Landesman**, "May we have the pleasure?", *The Guardian*, 17/10/1998

It was late May and I had gone to see my GP. Whilst I was waiting I couldn't help but notice a very interesting poster. It was the photograph of a table covered with various empty glasses of all shapes and colours which had apparently contained alcohol. In the background there was a Malaga-type resort and a beach. The poster was done by Health Care North West and it read:

IS THIS ALL YOU'RE GOING TO SEE ON HOLIDAYS?
DRINK WISELY AND HAVE A BETTER TIME.

I believe that the word "holiday" is not sufficient to convey the full significance of the term. It should be re-baptized as "alcoholiday"—hence the question "Is this all you're going to see on your alcoholidays?" would become absurd, as it appears to challenge a self-evident notion.

> What can save people from suicide, the drug *par excel-
> lence*, has always been some sort of cultural security.
> People who take drugs are culturally insecure.
>
> —**Pier Paolo Pasolini**, *Droga e Cultura, Il Caos*

> You'll never hope to stay within the "safe" number of
> units, and even the most conscientious of doctor would
> be surprised if you did—they were students once, and
> medics have the worst reputation of all.
>
> —*Sub Student Handbook*, p. 30

I've been lucky enough to become friendly with a group of medical students. And they've told me various stories. Like how doctors put themselves on the drip for ten minutes before they
start work in order to sober up after a night of debauchery. A
trainee doctor once recounted how he delivered a baby drunk.
One of the most interesting incidents, though, I witnessed in
person.

The hero was an aspirant medic in possession of a quantity of
adulterated amphetamine. It seems that somebody had told him
that amphetamines dissolve in vinegar and he was determined
to purify it. So he got a wine glass and filled it up to the middle
with vinegar. He added the powder, stirred and then drank it
while holding his nose!

> A country rector is the toast of his parishes after turning
> to drink to keep three churches alive.
>
> —*Rector turns to drink to save churches*,
> **The Manchester Metro News**, 9/8/1996

A modern saint. No doubt.

> Mr Broster cited historical precedence for his venture (...):
> "There has been a long association of churches brewing

beer. St Andrew's in Lewes brewed beer to mark the accession of Mary".

—*Rector turns to drink to save churches,*
The Manchester Metro News, 9/8/1996

I was wrong after all. You see, I had thought that the correlation between divine worship and yeast extract was a relatively new phenomenon. This new discovery goaded me into conducting further research wherein I discovered even stronger links between religion and alcohol. Indeed, I am informed that many aspects of religious life are closely linked with alcohol, *Holy Communion* being one of them: "Termly communion at Oxford in the regency period was a drunken occasion" (Brian Harrison, *Drink and the Victorians*, p. 43). Then we move to marriage: "Festive and economic arrangements at weddings reveal how, in remoter areas, religion, drink and the agricultural interest were closely integrated" (ibid., p. 43). And of course we shouldn't miss the most important event in one's life—death:

> Fatalistic escapism helps to explain the lavish drinking at funerals... Drab lives acquired dignity in death. Again relatives showed respect to the dead, as to the living, by ceremonially drinking.
>
> —**Brian Harrison**, *Drink and the Victorians*, p. 44

David Pitman, landlord of the Watermill public house in Burgess Hill, said: "It sells well and it is popular. It is a traditional ale and a damn good product. It is the nearest thing to God".

—**The Manchester Metro News**, 9/8/1996

Wow, sheer spirit-uality! Write for me not a chapter, but a *whole book* on the metaphysics of real ale consumption!

Or, perhaps, come up with an advertisement on the metaphysics of real ale consumption. Well, somebody has already spared us the trouble. It depicts two monks praying towards a delta-shaped stained-glass window in the centre of which there is the image of a pint with a halo around it. The caption goes:

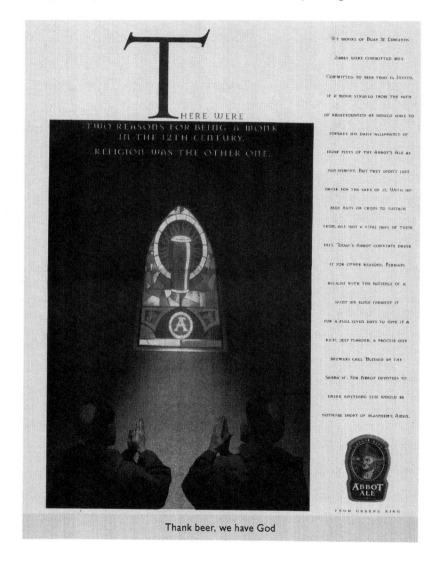

Thank beer, we have God

THERE WERE
TWO REASONS FOR BEING A MONK
IN THE TWENTIETH CENTURY.
RELIGION WAS THE OTHER ONE.

And the rest of the one-page ad read:

THE MONKS OF BURY St EDMUNDS
ABBEY WERE COMMITTED MEN.
COMMITTED TO BEER THAT IS. INDEED,
IF A MONK STRAYED FROM THE PATH
OF RIGHTEOUSNESS HE WOULD HAVE TO
FORSAKE HIS DAILY ALLOWANCE OF
EIGHT PINTS OF THE ABBOT'S ALE AS
PUNISHMENT. BUT THEY DIDN'T JUST
DRINK FOR THE SAKE OF IT. WITH NO
BEER NUTS OR CRISPS TO SUSTAIN
THEM, ALE WAS A VITAL PART OF THEIR
DIET. TODAY'S ABBOT CONVERTS DRINK
IT FOR OTHER REASONS. PERHAPS
BECAUSE WITH THE PATIENCE OF A
SAINT WE SLOW FERMENT IT
FOR A FULL SEVEN DAYS TO GIVE IT A
RICH, DEEP FLAVOUR; A PROCESS OUR
BREWERS CALL "BLESSED BY THE
SABBATH". FOR ABBOT DEVOTEES TO
DRINK ANYTHING ELSE WOULD BE
NOTHING SHORT OF BLASPHEMY. AMEN.

But I wouldn't let Abbot's Ale have the last word, notwithstanding the fact that it has been fermented for a "full seven days" (it takes as long to make Abbot's Ale as it took God to make the world and perhaps I shouldn't feel like waiting that long!), as I have been recently apprised of a major new discovery:

Carlsberg Tetley reveals a new product it calls "the holy grail of the drinks industry".

—*The Observer*, 1 September 1996

Now, after this, I can rest in peace. And so can this chapter.

The Doors of Perception

If the doors of perception were cleansed everything would appear to man as it is, infinite.

Aldous Huxley, *The Doors of Perception*

I was in my room, in the Halls of Residence, when I decided to taste this cow-dung grown "delicacy" that promised to deliver sounds, shapes, insights and altered states of consciousness, to say the least. They are colloquially known as *magic mushrooms* or *shrooms* and they can be any of a variety of hallucinogenic mushrooms species, i.e. *Psilocybe cubensis (boomers* or *gold caps)* or *Psilocybe semilanceata (liberty caps)*. I prepared a tea by boiling the mushrooms, pouring the liquid in my mug, and allowing a black tea sachet to infuse it in order to give it some flavour, or, more aptly, to obscure the not-so-pleasant taste of the mushroom brew. In about 15 minutes my stomach started to experience a slight unrest, as if it was trying to decide whether it should push my food all the way up to my mouth or not—nothing really to worry about, as it proved later.

When half an hour had passed, the unease had subsided beneath a rising feeling of unity, balance and well-being. One of the first things I noticed was a tree, whose branches were reaching up to my window. I had seen it before, of course. Somehow, though, this time was different. It was as if I was seeing it for the very first time. As if its essence had been evading me all along.

The leaves, the branches, and the tree became alive in a way I had never experienced before. *It dawned on me that the tree was a sentient being, bursting with life, as alive as me, or any human being, for that matter.*

Then I looked further off. I saw students walking by in utter misery, with the proverbial chip on their shoulders, sometimes accompanied by their equally afflicted parents (who would diligently check the smoke alarms in their offspring's new premises), whilst I was experiencing what I perceived as a *naturally blissful state of being.* I felt, deep inside, that life, as people were experiencing it, was a grand farce. On the one hand, all the bliss and love and affection at our fingertips, waiting to be seized upon; and on the other, people wallowing in a self-created mire of profound misery and alienation. *I was laughing and laughing and laughing—it was so sad that it was funny!*

The experience lasted about 4 hours, with diminishing intensity. It was undoubtedly the most profound spiritual experience of my life. I was able to have a glimpse of realities whose existence I could previously only surmise or perhaps read about in books. However, the integration of this kind of experience into everyday life was by no means an easy task for one who had no background in the practice of mindfulness and awareness (or what Eckhart Tolle aptly calls *presence*).

For some strange reason, this substance, in its dry form, is a *class A controlled drug* (i.e., in the same class as the extremely addictive and toxic substances heroin and cocaine), despite being totally non-addictive and having caused no documented deaths. For an instant I was perplexed. Alcohol and tobacco, two of the substances which were highly addictive and responsible for hundreds of thousands of deaths annually in Brutland, were sold legally almost everywhere (often "by appointment to Her Majesty the Queen"). They even had dedicated vending machines, so that the natives never had to worry about getting their fix. But then again, the state could make no profits from mushroom sale. Doctors, hospitals, clinics, pharmaceutical companies and the like would earn nothing in treating addicts, since *psilocybin*, the active substance, caused no addiction, no cancer, no heart disease or any other ailment that is typically caused by tobacco consumption.

In a bizarre way, it made sense. How would all these oath-of-Hippocrates-sworn professionals survive, if not through the death and suffering of others?

⁊🐋

I remember my first visit to *The Haçienda*, a well-known night-life establishment (labeled the most famous club in the world by *Newsweek* during the 1990s). For some strange reason *nobody was drinking any beer*, or for that matter, any alcohol at all. The customers were holding only small bottles of water. I was perplexed by this bizarre situation. *How could the natives survive without pints?* How could the club survive without the income generated from pint consumption?

When I further enquired, it transpired that they were consuming MDMA, colloquially known as *ecstasy* or *E*. MDMA is an "entactogenic" substance, from the roots *en* (Greek: within), *tactus* (Latin: touch) and *-gen* (Greek: produce). In other words, it produces feelings of empathy, love, interpersonal warmth and a desire to touch people, without the unsavoury side effects of alcohol (such as vomiting and violent behaviour).

After due consideration, I decided to ingest said substance—don't get me wrong, this was done strictly for research purposes. It was a white, dove-imprinted pill. Soon after ingestion, lo and behold, all inhibitions were gone! I felt at ease enough to go up to any girl and chat her up or hold her hands. Music and tempo became so intense and exhilarating, I could dance for hours non-stop (hence the need for frequent rehydration from the water bottles). Time seemed to pass at an amazing speed, and I could describe my state of being as nothing less than euphoric.

When the morning was drawing nigh, in the club's "chill-out" room, I had a major epiphany. *My life is shit but I don't give a shit*: this was the motto of a profound acceptance of my predicament that reverberated in my serotonin-enhanced neurons. The day after, there was no hangover, no funny comedown, no depression—just the quintessence of my epiphany, which slowly faded out of my life over the next few weeks.

Don't you just love it when mysteries are solved, people drink more water rather than beer, and less vomit is strewn upon the streets of Cloud*puku*land?

The Darlings of the System

British students believe there are no answers to anything. This prepares the British student to be indifferent to anything other than having a good time. "Work is a chore; it isn't cool to say that it actually *interests* you. Don't question, don't assert, don't argue".

—**Simon Schama** in **Rosa Ehrenreich**, *A Garden of Paper Flowers*, p. 196

A graduate ought to be self-motivated, and have acquired habits of study and concentration; have engaged with teaching and learning that themselves are informed by research and scholarship (try defining those).

But behind that lies a controversial idea: being a graduate means possessing an ability to criticize the status quo... a way of seeing things as they really are, a critical intellect. It somehow doesn't sound like a contemporary virtue...

To be a graduate means to have smoked the weed... before spending the entire corporate graduate induction programme denying you ever inhaled.

—*The Independent*, 7/12/1996, *Who knows what a graduate is? Discuss*

Alco-pop, pop music for alcoholics. As seen on Squirrel
(bar located within Owens Park Halls of Residence)

Students making the college scene for the first time can no longer afford to be zappy young things sleeping around campus in a self-induced daze.

They have one big dread and it isn't the kind that's cool to wear on their heads. It's money angst: how to fund some simple debauchery and stay out of debt. But instead of blaming strapped-for-cash universities and bungling governments, it's time the neophytes stopped passing the buck and totted up how much they spend on vices like hooch, cheroot and stash.

Student juicehounds will be £1,077 out of pocket after a year; clubbers will spend on average £480 a year; tripped out space cadets will fork out in excess of £ 960 on purple haze. Add all this up, and they will have spent more than £3,000 a year on their vices alone, more than the average debt, which, according to the NUS is £2,000 after the first year.

A better option for students to invest their drinking money is a Building Society savings account...

The amount paid each month can be changed if circumstances alter, for example, if extra dosh has to be dished out for a guzzling frenzy.

— "Students caught in the vice", *The Guardian*, 12/10/1996

Samantha: I'm starving! Where's the food?

Miranda: They're WASPs. There's never food, only booze.

Samantha: Fine. One martini, six olives

— **Sex and the City**, *All or Nothing*

*S*tudent life in Brutland starts with two things: Halls of Residence and beer. The former is the proper habitat, the *locus mirabilis* where a thousand and one manifestations of student life can flourish uninhibitedly.

Now, Halls of Residence is the *ne plus ultra* of repulsiveness. The epicentre of disgust is situated in the kitchen where one witnesses a fair accumulation of undisposed rubbish occupying the floor in the form of wheeley-bags, or, otherwise, in the form of free range, semi-putrefied garbage.

The sink and purlieus are under constant attack by a fleet of tomato-wounded crockery with the occasional emergence of intestinal (in smell and appearance) macaroni. The rule is that if one wants to eat, it will be impossible to obviate the necessity of resuscitating one of the tomato paste victims.

The *common room* exhibits a similar trademark condition. However, reasonable additions have been generously provided: shoes and socks abandoned by their owners in oblivious corners; cigarette butts which have had short but sizzling affairs with the carpet; and cassettes, videotapes, books, newspapers (mostly tabloids) and letters interspersed in a random fashion. Occasionally, rummaging through this amorphous pile of homogenised material, I could retrieve something of great anthropological curiosity, like a letter from somebody's mum which had joined the pile of trash, its topic being "the new car..." (it could have been the new leather sofa) "...that your dad bought".

🍃

At the end of the term, a few unfortunate individuals may have to stay on in order to achieve a state of inner contentment and self-worth; those persons, seemingly permitted to do so by the very structure of the Hall, perform the rite known as *fridge hunting*.

It is executed by means of a meticulous examination of the edible contents of the preserving apparatus, with special regard to items which have already expired (to avoid nauseous episodes unrelated to alcohol).

This activity can hardly bear significant material profit in terms of edible substances, but even the smallest of discoveries are conducive to a rush of adrenaline and an increase in serotonin levels. A literal outburst of serotonergic excretions occurs when the player has chanced upon any form or shape of liquid yeast extract container.

This is a game one plays solo and ASAP. Motto: All for one and one for himself.

The *Fenestral Cosmic Freeze*—as implemented by students pursuing a means of theft-proof refrigeration during their laborious sojourn in Halls, often by virtue of the semi-gratuitous assistance of the all-purpose Kwiksave carrier bag—represents one more victory of wholesome teenage spirit against gerontocratic technocracy. Not only does the fenestral method guarantee safety (provided you live on the second floor or above) thus helping dispense with insurance costs, but its advanced anti-freeze mechanism (the temperate outdoor climate) guarantees that you will never have to defrost it.

Festivals and pastimes are a common occurrence in Halls. One of them, which is very popular amongst the masculine population, is usually performed once as a celebration of entrance into the educational institution in question.

It is a game in which individuals have to maintain an able, repetitive, plentiful and (in terms of range) dynamic manipulation of their meat cylinder. It usually lasts for three days although sometimes it may last longer than that. The candidates are judged according to the aforementioned criteria and the winner is awarded paramount products of liquid yeast extract.

This game is called a *wankathon*.

In the Kingdom of Studentland, the King is nominated through a meritocratic tradition according to which prospective candidates are obliged to demonstrate their worthiness. That worthiness is judged by counting the number of liquid yeast extract-related nauseous episodes per year of the nominee.

Everybody in Studentland is very pleased with this system. You see, their life without a monarch would be a misery of boredom and national degradation; somehow it gives them a reason to live.

Student pop art: a beer wall and a traffic cone in a red brick background

The most salient totem in student culture is the omnipresent beer can. Students use them as decorative ornaments for their caves or hovels. Indeed, caves that have one or more of their walls covered with beer cans are envied by the rest of the community as paradigms of the popular sublime in artistic expression.

These are in fact proto-museums, prototypes of the contemporary museum.

≈

I would not want to pass on the mistaken belief that *beer walls* are the sole decorative item used by students. I should add that items of great decorative value for students can be found in the streets, a prime example thereof being *traffic cones* and *bollards* which are usually carried back home after a drunken spree. Indeed, I have tried hard to understand what it is exactly about these objects that captures their fascination but I only came up with questions and doubtful suppositions. Is it because they appropriate something that doesn't belong to them? Is it because the owner of the appropriated objects is the government? Is it because a "street look" enhances the macho image? Or is it simply one more tradition, another of the "things students do"?

≈

One thing about Britain's uncertain weather. We're a nation that's famous for inventing more indoor games than anyone else on earth.
—**Peter Cagney**, *The Book of Wit and Humour*, 1299

It seems that the favourite sport of the male of the species in its natural habitat—the so-called "Halls of Residence" or simply "Halls"—is indoor football and, in particular, the nocturnal version thereof played either in a duo or a solo (and in exceptional circumstances reaching a trio or a quartet). It is considered one of the major ways of venting frustration and alleviating a wide range of various other psychosomatic disorders that the male is particularly vulnerable to.

Another way of venting frustration is the pyromaniac routine undertaken by a number of natives on a "monkey see, monkey do" basis. Its most common expression is the incineration of papers affixed to notice boards in common areas.

Another noteworthy phenomenon pertaining to the series of phenomena that occur within the Halls of Residence context is the *Infinite Roll Accumulation* (IRA). This is the phenomenon according to which the native, after having performed the excremental functions and used up the hygienic paper (or *bog roll* as it is known in native speak), abjures the necessity of removing the empty cylinder. This results in the conspicuous multiplication of empty rolls in the small room which is the principal function room for scatological and processed liquid yeast extract discharging purposes. (And I say "principal" because the urinary function is commonly performed in private rooms that have the luxury of a sink).

My first reaction was to suppose a native acquaintance with existentialist doctrines—specifically, Sartre's theory of the morally and aesthetically debasing nature of the excremental function. But perhaps I was wrong. Indeed, I found no explanation for this behaviour, and, much to my chagrin, I was the one who continued collecting and disposing of them.

As part of my research I shared premises with a number of different native students in a number of different establishments.

Occasionally a bright, upstanding native would join forces with me. One of them, C. W., pinned up a note one day (a practice characteristic of native diplomacy in airing grievances):

Gentlemen

I shall be grateful if all members of the household will read this notice.

It is clear that one of the main reasons that this house is plagued with mice is due to the exceptionally poor standards of basic hygiene maintained by the people living here. If I may give an example, for most of this last week there were a number of plates, saucepans, cups, etc. left lying around in the living room which still contained significant quantities (for mice) of food. Indeed, when I took the trouble to wash up these items on Friday 18th there were mice droppings on some of the plates.

It seems entirely logical that one way in which the mice can be controlled is to deny them access to waste food. Therefore, we must ensure that plates etc. are not left lying around after meals and that any crockery, cutlery and pans are washed up as soon as is practicable after eating. (If you can't wash up, for whatever reason, then arrange with someone else to do it for you.)

If we continue to live like pigs then surely the mice will be followed by their good friends the rats.

Furthermore, for the smokers in the house, it should be remembered that plates and cups are not the appropriate places to dispose of ash and spent cigarettes. Picture it like this: would you like to eat your meals from an ashtray? Neither would I. There are an ample number of ashtrays about the house, please use them.

I am sure that there are many other points that can be raised, but these are the points of greatest concern to myself. I shall be grateful if you will heed the logic of my arguments.

Another item which indirectly describes and succinctly summarizes living conditions in Halls of Residence and student attitudes was an advert for Halls I found near Redbrick University:

FED UP?

With your student house
(or filthy students you live with)?
Can't cook, won't cook?
Crap social life?
Burgled one too many times?
Too far to walk to the nearest bar?

Then why not get a room in Owens Park... with all
facilities and catering included?

Indeed, it recommends moving into Halls and it makes a number of indirect assertions regarding the superiority of student life in Halls—assertions which have in the meantime been challenged. The only ones I could not refute were (a) the proximity to bars and (b) the fact that since it is catered you don't have to cook (of course that does not mean that the food is good or that you can eat whenever you like). When it comes to safety, things are indeed slightly better due to the presence of campus security, but nobody can really help much with the problems experienced from within:

> Students face a high risk of losing their most valued possessions in the first weeks of term... Sadly there is a rogue in all colleges... There is sometimes an element of easy come, easy go. When people share, they often find that items may be "borrowed" and never returned... Seasoned students living in rented accommodation are no less vulnerable... We've had incidents where people have bulldozed past students into their digs and stolen everything they can grab.
>
> —*The Observer*, 8/9/1996: "Take cover from thieves freshers told"

It should indeed be noted that the favourite pastime of the natives was a passive staring directed at the television (aka *telly*, other variants: *idiot box, goggle box, wobbly jelly*). It does, indeed, take the greatest part of their active time. As a function it is performed at a higher ritualistic level when it is accompanied by the consumption of the yellow liquid which is the result of the zymurgy of barley. It is at its highest and most respected when, as an adjunct to the liquid consumption, the theme stared at by the natives is football. It is so because it leads to a number of very interesting vocal utterances that find their unique expression exclusively on this occasion.

One special case of native behaviour was when one of them, after consuming his allotted can of yellow liquid from a big glass container (in native speak *pint*) would sneakily spit in it his excess saliva without the slightest compunction regarding the undercurrent of discontent that this could possibly rouse in his co-natives. However, they didn't seem to take much notice.

I am lucky in that Dr Silentiarius himself was involved in sharing premises with native students; he also ran the risk of being exposed, but thanks to his commitment to the sciences of anthropology and brutology he managed to survive in order to tell the tale. The following is another excerpt from his diary:

> The last few days I have come to notice an increased paranoia on the part of the natives. Although I have been living with them for a week, I have not partaken of their native practices such as consuming liquid yeast extract, watching pool and gladiators on TV, eating pizzas, falling unconscious in a club and expressing my sexuality and machismo with an eloquent stream of vomit.
>
> Is it possible that they've already sussed out than I'm an alien?

The females of the species that are more active in the domain of horizontal acrobatics find it useful to be rid of their bed and allow themselves only a mattress to sleep on, be it on their own or with various occasional partners—a wise move on their part, since Halls are hardly renowned for their soundproof architecture, let alone for their gossip-free denizens.

Students who have had to undergo an oppressive family unit regime do their best to ensure their admittance to an institution of higher education, where they can abandon the home unit and freely devote themselves to the liberating experience of divine worship in Yeast Extract Consumption Units. One can see their passionate devotion to religious duties in a pamphlet addressing the new additions to the parish (or *local* as the natives say), the so-called *freshers*:

Study carefully the health guidelines about safe consumption of alcohol, then rip it up. You'll never hope to stay within the "safe" number of units, and even the most conscientious of doctors would be surprised if you did— they were students once, and medics have the worst reputations of all.

Alcoholic students are common as Billy Bragg T-Shirts at an NF meeting; you'll never afford 10 pints a night all year, so give your liver a good workout in the first few weeks when your [sic] still feeling flush.

—The **SUB** Student Handbook, *p. 30*

It is common knowledge that even the most inept can achieve a male-to-female interface during the first few weeks. Those that fail in this task are individuals who shouldn't have much to expect in their lives anyway. However, the law of Brutland has it that *equal opportunities* should be everybody's right, be it in the professional, interpersonal, or advanced interpersonal (male-to-female) sphere:

The SUB Student Handbook is... given out free to new students in the City, although it's not as if they don't get enough free stuff already what with "Welcome Packs", cheap beer and easy sex. The Handbook will not print anything that discriminates on the grounds of sex, sexuality or people who can't get laid during freshers' week.

—The **SUB** Student Handbook, *p. 5*

And indeed, students are duly rewarded for their putative contribution to society, their against-the-grain individuality (one of the numerous examples is the student upheaval at the London School of Economics in 1969), their progressive nature full of new ideas and novel ways of improving individual as well as collective existence:

> And it's all for you, yes, you sir with the Inspiral Carpets
> T-Shirt and the sheepish look.
>
> —**The SUB Student Handbook**, p. 5

One can easily deduce from the above that, as Lemmy says:

> There'll never be another revolution in this country as
> long as you've got a hole in your arse.
>
> —*GQ*, December 1996, p. 230

Indeed, alcohol and drug abuse is a fixture of student life in Brutland. I have known quite a few students who spend much more money on booze than on food. They would eat sandwiches and No-Frills baked beans and they would manage with spending 20 quid per week for food whilst the expenses for booze would sometimes exceed 50 pounds—roughly 25 pints. And this evaluation applies to those who do not take any drugs at all. If drugs come into play the figures change dramatically: we could have a combined booze and drug expenditure that is twenty (or more) times higher than the amount of money spent on food.

And, as it transpired, I was not that wrong in my subjective evaluation of the native students' drinking habits:

> "Cigarettes and Alcohol" could be the decade's anthem.
> One in eight young men drinks to excess, sinking more
> that 50 units of alcohol each week, while nearly half
> broke the government's old safe drinking recommenda-
> tion... 42% of young men aged 18-24 drink more than 21
> units of alcohol per week—the highest proportion ever.
>
> —*Athens News*, 28/3/1998

What do southern European students usually do just after an exam? They go for a coffee. What do British students usually do just after an exam? They go for pints... *en masse*. I will never forget seeing students staggering and vomiting at three o' clock in the afternoon.

Apparently it is the best way to celebrate their newly-fledged freedom from lectures; nay, it is the best way to celebrate, anyway, anything!

Of course, boozing has been a proof of masculinity in Brutland from time immemorial. I will never forget the story told by a Greek undergrad who shared a flat in Halls with a group of six English guys. They had all gone out for a night *on the booze* and when they got back the Greek student was so *wasted* that he had to *puke* a number of times. The day after, his flatmates not only congratulated him on his achievement but also boasted about their flat having "real men"! If you find it hard to believe that this is a very common attitude, read on:

> This morning I awoke with my head in the fridge, the kettle had melted out on the stove and I had vomit in the turnups of my trousers. What a smashing Beer Festival!
>
> —**A. M.**'s letter to *Grip* (UMIST University students' magazine), 30/10/1996, p. 11

I think he deserves a silver medal for his achievements, and the writer of the following article deserves the gold one—or vice versa?

> And despite football hooligans, teenage alcoholics, and the British excesses on the various Costas del Drunkenness, we win Silver for National Sobriety.
>
> —GQ, December 1996, p. 224

So you think that what I am describing is perhaps only student life in some poxy Northern University? Well, that's not quite so. What do others think of the more prestigious institutions?

> She [Rosa Ehrenreich] found the [Oxford] undergraduates vapid, spotty, aimless and drunken. (...)
>
> She expected to enter a sophisticated factory for the making of complicated machinery to power space-flights. Instead, it turned out tins of cat-food.
>
> —The Times, 27/12/1994

You think Cambridge could be better? Lets see what the inmates say:

> We have sex (admittedly not very much, but at least it is more than Oxford), we take drugs (and consequently have higher debt expectations)...
>
> Overall, sex is something the Cambridge students do remarkably little of...
>
> Scarily, especially for such a supposedly intelligent community, more than half of the non-virgins here say that they have had unprotected sex, and of those nearly half say they are not worried by the prospect of AIDS.
>
> —The Times, 7/12/1996:"Drugs and debts but not much of a sex life",
> "Cambridge view": By Imogen Wall, Editor of Varsity.

And back to Oxford:

> Passion is to be avoided; intellectual and political passions are sources of shame, not pride, and wise students hide all such passions from their peers.
>
> —**Rosa Ehrenreich**, A Garden of Paper Flowers, p. 192

Indeed, if the above statements regarding Oxbridge hold true, then try to visualize what the other campuses are like! Instantly, the words of Nietzsche spring to mind, and the way he described the German intellect now seems like a valid description of the Anglo-Saxon intellect in general:

> How much dreary heaviness, lameness, dampness, slop-piness, how much *beer* there is in the German intellect! How can it possibly happen that young men who dedicate their existence to the most spiritual goals lack all sense of their first instinct of spirituality, *the spirit's instinct for self-preservation*—and drink beer? ... passion in spiritual things is more and more on the decline.
>
> —**Friedrich Nietzsche**, *Twilight of the Idols*: "What the Germans lack".

And since we are talking about spiritual things and beer, per-haps I should quote a native clergyman's opinion on the matter:

> What two ideas are more inseparable than beer and Britannia?
>
> —**Sydney Smith**, Hesketh Pearson, *The Smith of Smiths*, ch. 11 (1934).

It is true however, that you can find great scholars in this coun-try, great scholars—who will not possess any spirit at all. Looking back on my freshman fantasies regarding academic life, I cannot help but laugh at my naivety. Not only was I expecting that I would find intellectuals who would see the society and the world they were born in with a critical eye, but also, *with even more fervour*, I was hoping to find *spirituality*. Perhaps I was a tad too idealistic in seeing myself as a *homo universalis* comfortably ensconced in my Renaissance utopia. Later on, I discovered that spirituality is hard enough to come by in monasteries, let alone in universities. But after all, who am I to criticize students who were just looking for some action, and all they managed to find was chemical distraction?

Beer and bank—what do they have in common?

Overdraught

Doggedness is an essential part of the British personality, but it needs the complement of ruthlessness to be
effective.
—**Peter Grosvenor & James McMillan,** *The British Genius,* p. 16

he term *overdraft* is one more of the keywords of student life. (Even a pub has caught up on the idea and
called itself "Overdraught" alluding to the two main priorities of
student life: beer and how to pay for it.) I know hardly any student who during his studies didn't have to take an overdraft at
least once. It is an allowance made for the "darlings of the system" so that they will be more docile and disciplined (and *tax-rid-
den*) during the rest of their (hopefully) working lives. However,
things are not as simple as they may seem. Normally, you think
that banks (according to their ads) give you a limit of more or
less £1000 interest-free overdraft. What they *don't* tell you, however, is that in order to be eligible for it you have to *formally apply*
for one. Indeed, if you don't do so, then you will not simply be
daft, but *overdaft*, as once you get into the process of so-called
unauthorised borrowing, you are liable for *administration fees* of
about £25 per cheque. To make it simple, let's say you have signed
three cheques for £5 each and you are left with no money in
your account without having made any overdraft arrangements.
As a result of this you will be charged £75 administrative fees for
your negligence. Not to say they're ruthless, but the fact of your
being only a poor student is not really of much interest to them:

The letter was headed FINAL NOTICE and stated his outstanding balance was £778.36. It continued: "Unless full settlement is made immediately your account will be placed in the hands of a Professional Debt Collection Agency.

When his sister phoned the bank she was told that he could have paid his debt by paying a pound per week, something which, of course, was not mentioned in their threatening letter. Notably, his overdraft was far below the average student overdraft which, for the year 1996, was £1,982. Furthermore, studies by the NUS have shown that university students aged between 22 to 26 have an average debt of £4,301".

—*The Express*, 16/1/1997
"Student, 22, hangs himself over debt threat"

There is only one way to deal with banks and their threats (and this could be applied to many other services in Brutland). What you have to do is *keep in touch with them*, ring them, write to them, pop by, and constantly reassure them that you are mindful of the situation and that you are doing your best to resolve it.

However, banks are there so that you can get the most out of them whilst you are still a student. Don't forget that they will be enjoying a fat income once you get that well-paying job. And, of course, they won't give you an account of how they invest *your* money, whereas when you are taking an overdraft you frequently have to fill out a form listing your detailed expenses and often you are asked with something more than just a *soupçon* of suspicion, "what do you want the money for?' (tell them: "for educational material"), because, you see, you have committed the greatest of crimes, the crime of experiencing *cashflow difficulties*—the crime of *being a student*.

In the Groves of Academe

The race of prophets is extinct. Europe is becoming set in its ways, slowly embalming itself beneath the wrappings of its borders, its factories, its law-courts and its universities. The frozen Mind cracks between the mineral staves which close upon it. The fault lies with your mouldy systems, your logic of $2 + 2 = 4$. The fault lies with you, Chancellors, caught in the net of syllogisms. You manufacture engineers, magistrates, doctors, who know nothing of the true mysteries of the body or the cosmic laws of existence. False scholars blind outside this world, philosophers who pretend to reconstruct the mind. The least act of spontaneous creation is a more complex and revealing world than any metaphysics.

—**Antonin Artaud**
Letter to the Chancellors of the European Universities

The general quality of teaching [at Oxford] is dismally low... lecturers should vary their tone, make eye contact with the audience, stand up while lecturing, speak audibly, make sure lectures have a clear organizational structure, and encourage students to ask questions about points that are not clear... there is no institutionalised recognition for students who have taken the trouble to go beyond the basics and pursue their own intellectual interests. It creates very narrow students.

—**Rosa Ehrenreich**, *A Garden of Paper Flowers*, p. 232

Oxford micromanages student lives when it comes to rules about gowns, examinations, mealtimes, and so on. But when it comes to the big issues—how shall we live together? How shall we create an atmosphere in which people can learn and thrive?—Oxford is strangely silent. The dons seem to regard these as irrelevant concerns, and students follow their lead.
—**Rosa Ehrenreich**, *A Garden of Paper Flowers*, p. 241

Not only do universities function mainly to socialize students for the values of the corporate economy; but even more seriously the assumed "stability" of this set-up is nothing but a hoax. Ever since World War II, the economics, communication media, government, and values of the West have been dominated, at an ever increasing rate, by gigantic corporate monoliths, the spectacular beneficiaries of the international arms race.
—**P. Hoch & V. Schoenbach**, *LSE: The Natives are Restless*, Introduction, p. xi

This "demystification" process is an essential first step in transforming the universities from training and socialising machines for the status quo into spawning grounds for opponents of the system. Until students see examinations as the means of forcing them to learn what the system wants them to, rather than what is relevant or even correct; until they see professors as the foremen ("supervisors") of the training process, rather than people searching after "truth"; until they see the university itself as a plush version of an infant's school, rather than a place where the values and institutions of society may be questioned—until then they will not be able to mount a struggle to transform this system.
—*ibid.*, pp. 193-4

In England, at any rate, education produces no effect whatsoever. If it did, it would prove a serious danger to the
upper classes, and would probably lead to acts of violence in
Grosvenor Square.

—**Oscar Wilde**, *The Importance of Being Earnest*

here I was, at 17 years of age, with no A-levels, having flown to Brutland from Greece, in order to attend an interview at the University of the Laughingshire with respect to a course in creative suffering. Well, there hadn't been much of an interview, the guy just asked whether I had studied any literary criticism before at school and how long it would take me to read a Dickens novel, to which I replied: "About a week, two weeks, depending on how big it is".

Then he thought that there were alternative opportunities for me called "Colleges of Higher Education" and he drew a map for me on the blackboard indicating where exactly were the inter-national airports in the cities possessing these institutions so that I could travel to and from my country.

To console me he also said that if I sat an A-level in Creative Suffering and managed to score C or above he would take me on the course next year. I enquired whether he could give me a copy of the reference I had in my application to use it as an open reference for other Universities or "Colleges of Higher Education" and he was shocked: "Oh, I couldn't do that, that's confidential information!". At the end he said the most he could do for me was ring up that "chap" (well, it was a woman) in order to get permission (there was no answer).

The following year I sat two A-levels, one in Creative Suffering (scoring the sought-after "C") and another one scoring "A". And despite the fact that I reapplied, I never heard from that man again.

Well, now I remember another thing, "How much would you pay for a house in your neck of the woods?" he asked me. "Probably about £40.000", I said, "Well, to buy a decent place here you have to pay £200.000.' I believe that was the most motivated question he ever asked me, much more so than the one about Dickens. It had real passion in it.

Why should Morris Zapp, who always claimed that he had made himself an authority on the literature of England not in spite of but *because* of never having set foot in the country, why should he of all people suddenly join the annual migration to Europe?

—**David Lodge**, *Changing Places*, p. 39

But there is no literary public in England for anything except newspapers, primers and encyclopaedias. Of all people in the world the English have the least sense of the beauty of literature.

—**Oscar Wilde**, *The Picture of Dorian Gray*

I almost feel nostalgic when I recollect the times of my first degree, my BA in Creative Suffering: my memories have been beautified by temporal distance. I should not forget, however, that I am one of those people who tend to beautify the past even if it has been rather unsightly. Nevertheless, I cannot resist the temptation to quote the last few paragraphs of a piece of assessed coursework I had to submit for my degree (i.e., my final two-thousand-five-hundred-word essay). It is all about *meaning* in an age of meaninglessness:

Now, the wheel has come full circle as I have attempted to explain my apparently cryptic and irrelevant glosso-theological introduction. As we have seen from the foregoing, the concept that lies hidden between the Saussurian dichotomy discussed herein, is one with the highest degree of semantic volatility and inflammability—*meaning*. So, I shall finalize my argument by reaching the tip of my inverted semantic pyramid—hopefully without invoking the assistance of *les pompiers*.

Thus, the only retort to the vain logomachy about "meaning" in language and literature can be given by means of the Doctrine of Excremental Anti-Fallacy (DEAF). This doctrine has been postulated and endorsed by many highly established and venerable figures of the literary academia. Beginning with Antonin Artaud ("All writing is pigshit") and continuing with old toad Larkin ("books are a load of shit"), one could prolong this paradigmatic discourse *ad infinitum;* the only thing adding variation would be the quality, source, and obscenity of the excremental substance in question.

Perhaps, more idiosyncratic could be Beckett's case: his DEAF would probably contain the epithet pink.

Merde, c'est finis... vamos a la playa!

P.S. As Bertolt Brecht says: "It is a misfortune having to live in a country in which there is no humour. It is even a greater misfortune, however, if you live in a country in which you need humour to survive".

The third institute of higher education I experienced, this time for postgraduate studies, was the University of Moral Integrity and Sacred Tradition where I specialized in Psychological Engineering. A great fear of the University of Moral Integrity and Sacred Tradition is that its sex-of-the-art electronic equipment may be used by its students for immoral purposes. Students who would go to such an extreme of vulgarity as to "conduct their love lives" through the respected university's machinery would be firstly castrated (or clitoridectomised in the case of the subject being female), and then stoned to death by fellow students and members of the staff.

Indeed, this fundamental principle was painstakingly instilled into the students' malleable brains from their very first day at the University through constant reminders of the temperatures that prevailed amid the raging fires of hell.

Thus, the university's department of Psychological Engineering (previously known as "Psychology and Psychiatry") fulfilled to the maximum its didactic purpose.

§

Perhaps the funniest incident during my time in a native establishment of higher education occurred when I (and I believe everybody else as well) thought that our linguistics teacher was claiming during a lecture on English dialectology that she had "erotic accent". Most students managed quite well at hiding a grin, but, although they were puzzled, nobody dared challenge this notion which had found its expression in a most inappropriate environment. Only a few minutes later was the mystery solved when she added, "You see I pronounce my post-vocalic *r*s". Of course she did, what did you expect, every Scot has a rhotic accent!

§

It was not until some years later, when I was already gone from Brutland, that I read a book which expressed so well this nausea that the local academia inspired in me:

> I speak of these divagations of his [Seferiadis'] because they were a refreshing antidote to the sort of obsessive, single-tracked and wholly mirthless order of conversation indulged in by the English literati in Athens. An evening with these buttery-mouthed jakes always left me in a suicidal mood. A Greek is alive to the finger tips; he oozes vitality, he's effervescent, he's ubiquitous in spirit. The Englishman is lymphatic, made for the arm-chair, the fireside, the dingy tavern, the didactic treadmill. Durrel used to take a perverse delight in observing my discomfiture in the presence of his countrymen: they were one and all like animated cartoons from his Black Book, that

devastating chronicle of the English death. In the presence of an Englishman Katsimbalis would positively dry up. Nobody really hated them—they were simply insufferable.

—**Henry Miller**, *The Colossus of Maroussi*, p. 110

A Welcoming Kipper, or the Art of Sodomy

Kipper: Of an English person, usually male. Visiting Aus., became very nice about everything while he is there, and then, back in England writing "nasty little things" that he failed to mention while among the people whose hospitality he accepted. This unlovable trait has led to the application of the expression kipper to a certain type of Englishman. A kipper, by virtue of the processing, has become two-faced "with no guts".

  —**Eric Partridge**, *A dictionary of slang and unconventional English*, p. 648

Sodomy is another oft-uncorrected misconstruction; most biblical scholars now say that the sin of Sodom was not pederasty but inhospitality to strangers.

  —*The Independent*, 11/11/1996

A young and attractive lady is invited here. Her luggage is left on the steps for hours; and she herself is deposited in the poop and abandoned, tired and starving. This is our hospitality. These are our manners. No room ready. No hot water. No welcoming hostess. Our visitor is to sleep on the toolshed, and to wash in the duckpond.

  —**George Bernard Shaw**, *Heartbreak House,* Act I, The Captain

The faculty began to trickle back to their posts. From behind his desk he heard them passing in the corridor, greeting each other, laughing and opening and shutting their doors. But when he ventured into the corridor himself they seemed to avoid him, bolting into their offices just as he emerged from his own, or else they looked straight through him as of he were the man who serviced the central heating. Just when he had decided that he would have to take the initiative by ambushing his British colleagues as they passed his door at coffee-time and dragging them into his office, they began to acknowledge his presence in a way which suggested long but not deep familiarity, tossing him a perfunctory smile as they passed, or nodding their heads, without breaking step or their conversations. This new behaviour implied that they all knew perfectly well who he was, thus making any attempt at self-introduction on his part superfluous, while at the same time it offered no purchase for extending acquaintance. Morris began to think that he was going to pass through Rummidge English Department without anyone actually speaking to him. They would fend him off for six months with their little smiles and nods and then the waters would close over him and it would be as if he had never disturbed their surface.

—**David Lodge**, *Changing Places*, p. 59

A LOLLIPOP lady who refused to help two foreign schoolboys is to go back on duty after a reprimand. Jean Turner, of Barnstaple, north Devon, told the two 10-year-olds from Eastern Europe, who were in Britain to learn about the English way of life: "I only help the English kids".

—*The Times*, 11/6/1995, "Sour taste: Jean Turner, Lollipop Lady" (Ireland)

If they are stupid enough to look on the wrong side of the road before they cross it, then they deserve absolutely no help from me. As Darwin says: "natural selection", or even, "the survival of the fittest".

Indeed, the plethora of racially offensive terms in the English language doesn't really come as a surprise, reflecting as it does the xenophobic attitude of the natives. In fact, English seems to contain more terms of racial abuse that nearly any other language.

And to substantiate my sayings I will quote some of them. The following are used for black people: *coon, darkie, dinge, egg and spoon* (rhyming slang for *coon*), *nigger, spade, Lucozade* (rhyming slang for *spade*), *nignog, soap dodger, stove lid, smoke, wog,* etc.

However, black people are not the only ones who suffer: The Frenchman is called *frog*; the Chinese, *Chink, Chinky, tiddleywink*; the German, *boche, kraut, Fritz, jerry, squarehead*; the Greek, *bubble and squeak*; the Pakistani, *paki*; the Jew, *yid*; the Argentinian, *argie*, etc. Of course, we there are also umbrella terms covering groups of foreigners like *dago*, which describes people of Latin origin (Italians, Spanish, Portuguese), and *PIGS* which stands for Poles, Italians, Greeks, Slavs. The list is by no means exhaustive and a lookup in a slang thesaurus will give you many more of these little gems.

And it should not come as a surprise to anybody that a series of small anthropological guides to the various peoples of the earth was published in Brutland with the title: *Xenophobe's Guides*.

Methinks that the *Xenophobe's Guide to the English* needs to be upgraded in order to inform foreign students who might go there without the least idea of what this xenophobia thing is all about:

> Foreign students who go to... Weymouth to learn English this summer will have a new lesson on their curriculum—how to survive the attentions of violent local teenagers.

I can understand that: if you're not English, why go to England? You're surely asking for trouble...

> We will ask the hoteliers on the seafront to display a logo in their front windows which will tell the students this is somewhere they will not be turned away from if they come looking for help.

Ahh-hah, this is a BIG sign of hospitality—one need not search any further for a more exhaustive definition of this elusive concept.

> "I can't stand them personally although I think its wrong to do them any harm. Other tourists I don't mind but this place gets crammed with kids who don't speak the language and are away from home looking for a good time. I think they are partly at fault", said a local, Keith Russell.
>
> —*The Guardian*, 31/5/1996

Well, look at the English tourists, they are all mobile multilingual tools—I haven't yet met an English tourist who doesn't have at his fingertips the visiting country's language. I'm telling you, these people are polyglots born and bred.

To prove my assertions on the linguistic superiority of the natives I shall have to quote some statistics that relate to their immaculate performance:

John Gordon, of the University of East Anglia, reports soberly that of a recent intake of undergraduates reading German a mere eight out of 43 could translate the sentence "The teacher gave the pupil the book" into German. Only four could manage "I prefer to drink strong coffee".

— *The Times*, "Parlez-vous Franglais?", 15/11/1996

Inability to speak foreign languages seems to be the major, if not the only, intellectual achievement of the average Englishman.

— **George Mikes**, *How to be a Brit*, p. 161

Dress English, speak English, act English or go home.

— Signed: "BNP" (lavatorial graffito at Redbrick University)

It makes sense (partially, that is): there is no harm done by speaking English.

Despite the fact that it is not really necessary—remember, all English are polyglots, whoops! sorry, I actually meant *omniglots*: they automatically speak the language of the country they are in, only by virtue of physically being there!

And of course I can back up this assumption. I was surprised by the fact that ordinary students in Brutland exhibited a remarkable knowledge of defunct languages whilst in a pub—something which sounded very promising for their knowledge of contemporary languages. After a few hours of debauchery I started noticing people falling unconscious on the floor (I remember a native once mentioning in a pre-outing discussion that he is going to get "bloody unconscious" but I could not understand what he meant.)

It all started to make sense though when I noticed the writing on the pub wall:

USQUE AD MORTEM BIBENDUM
[Lets drink until death]

And of course, when they go abroad they are so amicable to everybody else—it's just that they don't want to show it! Now I understand my flatmate when he describes his own people as harbouring "an unspoken ill feeling for all other countries":

> In high season [Skiathos] is crowded with Italians and Germans but by early September they have gone, taking their video cameras with them, *and good riddance*, so September and October is a good time to visit. [My emphasis]

—*The Times*, 7/9/1996

Indeed, *anything* coming from abroad is evil. And this brings to mind a campaign against Europe with the motto "Brussels sprouts" (referring to how unwelcome EC directives are). I think I know what lies behind that. There are rumours that the main reason behind Britain's veto of the euro is the fact that the government is preparing to launch a new national currency unit which will bear the code name *pint*. One of the main arguments put forth in the House of Lords in favour of the introduction of this new currency is that it will greatly facilitate the everyday transactions of the drinking classes.

A pint's a pound, the world around.

—*Old mnemonic saw*

Experience teaches that it is not easy to have the English take any notice of you. Often they don't even bother about natural disasters, such as their climate... Maria Edgeworth... makes the matter clear, when alluding to the earthquake "which had the honour to be noticed by the English Royal Society".

—**Idries Shah**, *The Natives Are Restless*, p. 85

In Brutland, exoticism, the novelty value, doesn't really work, as people lack any intellectual or emotional curiosity about what goes on in other people's brains or hearts. You don't really stand a chance of being noticed...

unless of course you are Italian and the native in question is female.

§

I've been told off for smiling when I show the red card.
[Wendy Toms, the first woman to referee a professional match in Britain.]
— *The Guardian*, 28/12/1996
("The Year in Review" by Catherine Bennett)

For Cambridge people rarely smile,
Being urban, squat, and packed with guile.

—**Rupert Brooke**, *The Old Vicarage, Grantchester*

It was said that a native could be trained to say "hello" after a year of uninterrupted acquaintance. Some people went as far as claiming that in a few decades you could get them to force their facial muscles into a smile for a bit longer than five nanoseconds.

But these were nothing but unfounded rumours. The only type of smile I witnessed was a cross between a smile and a sneer, a stultified lip-curl of embarrassment or half-concealed arrogance. There is still quite a lot of work that needs to be done on each one of the fourteen individual muscles that are necessary in order to smile. However, the science of Anglosaxon Lip Manipulation is still at an embryonic stage—further developments eagerly awaited.

I remember the first time I visited Brutland. I was seventeen and everything had a fairytale-like texture. A brave new world of quaint housing—homogeneity was a plus at the time—, beautiful countryside and amazing libraries. One of the things, though, that I found most discordant with my home culture was the fact that when going to a party you had to bring your own booze! (Later I found out that the abbreviation "b.y.o.b." was a standard term which referred to this practice).

Back home, if a person is celebrating, you buy a gift for him or her, which could even be a bottle of whisky or something— but you never bring your own whiskey with you, let alone save it only for yourself!

If I were to suggest a cultural equivalent in the usage of abbreviations I would dare say that *b.y.o.b.* is the much sought equivalent of the French *R.S.V.P.,* just as *innit* should become the formal equivalent of *n'est-ce pas.*

☙

The following is another rare extract from the meagre remains of Dr Silentiarius' diaries during the Onanistan years:

> Yesterday went to a club of Redbrick called 42nd Street. Had my tongue bitten by a bitch when I tried to snog her—earnestly hoping to exercise my newly acquired Tongue Kung Fu skills. "Why did you do it?", I asked her. "Because I'm a bitch", she answered, in a fit of self-knowledge unusual in tongue-biting female hyenas. As I got up this morning my tongue still hurt. Drinking my tea was such a painful, drawn-out business that it reminded me of the times I was pissing as slowly as death, desperately trying to contain the pain that was caused by haemorrhagic inflammation of the urinal passage. By Jove, this *is* the heart of darkness!

Goodness and wisdom to the vile seem vile;
Filths savour but themselves.

—Albany in **William Shakespeare's** *King Lear,* Act IV, sc. ii. 38

But English gratitude is always such,
To hate the hand which doth oblige too much.

—**Daniel Defoe,** *The True-Born Englishman,* Part 2, 867-8

Soon after I had moved into Halls of Residence and was sharing a house with seven natives, strange things started happening that seemed to defy a series of natural laws: the milk tended to evaporate, the cheese to shrink, the mushrooms to fly out of the fridge—not that I personally witnessed such unorthodox phenomena (and at times I even thought that there might be some correlation with the weather), or had the slightest idea of how they could have taken place.

It remained an enigma until one day, in my readings of Marx and Engels, I chanced upon the fact that Engels himself had visited Redbrick during the industrial revolution. In fact, he lived in a house whose top storey is now a Hall of Residence; there he had his first revolutionary conceptions regarding an uprising of the working class. Suddenly, the whole universe regained its composure, and I regained my shattered confidence in the laws of physics. It was simple: I was living in a commune, sharing lodgings with true-blue comrades, direct descendants of the glorified Engelian lineage—proto-communism revisited!

However, in the recesses of my rational mind, so overwhelmed by this joyous discovery of native solidarity, there were still some niggling doubts: I had to put my assumption to the test. And the test consisted simply in allowing myself to share their comestibles the same way I welcomed them to share mine. But I didn't: it was, I felt, incumbent upon my culinary self-respect to avoid consuming processed foods and especially low quality meat products. And, I believe, sensitive as they were, they perceived this, and kindly refrained from offering the occasional No-Frills pork sausage or even a masterly prepared feast of beans on toast.

So, to this moment in time, I'm still unsure as to whether they were of leftish inclinations or not. One thing I know, though, is that they did have good taste, as they preferred my food to theirs, despite the fact that they were rather unacquainted with the possibly disconcertingly exotic Mediterranean cuisine. Ah, brave lads!

> People are strange, when you're a stranger, faces look
> ugly, women seem wicked, when you're alone.
> When you're strange, faces come out of the rain... when
> you're strange.

> —**Jim Morrison and The Doors**

Another entry from the diary of Dr Silentiarius, to serve as a reminder that an anthropologist is a cross-breed between a poet and a scientist:

Travelling Abroad
(Or the loneliness of the long distance traveller)

In my repeated vain attempts
to grasp through gestures
—loving gestures, gestures of pure
transcendence—
essence, ungraspable:

beyond the other's skin
a foreign country
and me—*exiled?*

But how can anybody be welcoming to people when failing to be welcoming to their proper emotions? Foreign people in Brutland are often stigmatised for unwanted emotions and are silently treated with contempt, disdain, formality, and phlegmaticism. Excommunication doesn't always have to be an overt process. *However,*

> great allowances should be given to a *Nation* who lives secluded from the rest of the world, and must therefore be altogether unacquainted with the Manners and Customs that most prevail in other nations: The want of which Knowledge will ever produce many *Prejudices*, and a certain *Narrowness of Thinking*; from which we and the politer Countries of *Europe* are wholly exempted.
>
> —*Jonathan Swift*, "Voyage to Brobdingnag", (*Gulliver's travels*, chapter VII)

Indeed:

> It will be no meagre subscription to a better tomorrow if British can transmit that calm instinct for decency to less favoured lands.
>
> —**Peter Grosvenor & James McMillan**,*The British Genius*, p. 189

"A Friend is a Quid"

Friendship, th' abstracted Union of the Mind,
Which all men seek, but very few can find:
Of all the Nations in the Universe,
None talk on't more, or understand it less:
For if it does their property annoy,
Their Property their Friendship will destroy.
> —**Daniel Defoe**, *The True-Born Englishman*, Part 2, 572-7

He's only got three friends in the world. And when that three quid's gone he doesn't know what he'll do...
> —**Peter Cagney**, *The Book of Wit and Humour*, No 574

*O*nce, I had a friend. Or should I say, he once had me. He was a very friendly chap from Scouseland. He was different, he wanted to share things with me. He seemed to like sharing things. He even wanted to share the thing closest to his heart with me: his *dope*. He would smoke his *spliffs* any time of the day, anywhere—even on the top deck of double-decker busses. Sometimes he would spend hours after a smoke watching tennis on television. Or snookers. Or even darts. When asked "What have you done today?" he would answer, *bugger-all, man* or (the occasional elegant variation) *fuck-all, man*.

One day he asked for a loan. He wanted a tenner, he said, and although I was not in the best of fiscal conditions, I did give it to him, gladly. Well, he *was* a friend of mine after all, wasn't he?

Next time I bumped into him he seemed to pass over me as if I were a stranger. I was perplexed. I even thought he might wear disposable contact lenses and have run out of fresh pairs; so I was willing to accept it with only the hint of a tear. Yet thereafter, to confirm my worst fears, on every single occasion where our ways seemed to cross, the same behaviour would repeat itself. Or rather the same non-behaviour. It dawned on me that I wouldn't really "see" him ever again. However, I missed him for a long time afterwards. You see, for me, he was still my friend.

To conclude: I shouldn't grumble; at least I learned something. I found out what a friendship is worth in this neck of the woods: *ten pounds*, or, to put it in real-life terms—(approximately) *a sixteenth of an ounce of dope.*

❧

I had met a woman (I wouldn't say "girl" because it would not be *politically correct*) who was part of a Christian group that spend time studying the Bible and, of course, attending Mass. One day we had arranged to go to the theatre together and our meeting place would be a few hundred yards away from the theatre. She arrived on time but she remembered that she had no money and, consequently, would have to go to the nearest cashpoint in order to get some. I said:

"Don't worry, you don't have to do that; anyway it's already 7:25 and the play starts at 7:30", and I gave her a fiver.

"Oh, I'm surprised, you *trust me!*" she exclaimed,

"Well, it's only money", I retorted.

After that a short existentialist discussion ensued, during which arose the critical moment when she had to pop the question:

"*Are you* a Christian?", she interrogated with a very serious expression in her face as if all depended upon my answer...

The play was rather crap (it was a modern version of Romeo and Juliet with Juliet wearing a revealing, clubby dress and the whole cast occasionally breaking into rave dancing) and I could not possibly tolerate the second part, so I apologised and left.

I never saw the Christian lady again.

❧

> "Don't you think", Melanie was saying, "that we have to aim towards a whole new concept of interpersonal relationships based on sharing rather than owning? I mean, like a socialism of emotions..."
>
> —**David Lodge**, *Changing Places*, p. 109

The following is a discussion between a young couple that had been living together for four years:

> She: I want to make a phone call.
> He: Why don't you do it then?
> She: I haven't got any change.
> He: Well, I could lend you some money.

> She: Are you sure? I only need 10p. I'll give it back to you tomorrow.

※

Speaking of money, I cannot help remembering that wonderful health food shop right in the middle of Redbrick's Studentland. It sold some wonderful pastries and pies (among which was Mediterranean pastry with spinach and feta cheese) and it also dabbled as a restaurant. What was peculiar about it was not quality. Nor prices—which were the ones you'd expect in such a place. That which struck me as quite unusual, to say the least, was the fact that the wonderful take away food I enjoyed so much, which was not exactly cheap, had two different prices. In other words, my favourite Mediterranean pastry would cost me 65p or 72p. How on earth is it possible? Well, it is not possible on earth, but it is possible in Redbrick. It's simple: as it is it costs 65p. If you want it hot, though (which actually means lukewarm as it only spends a few seconds in the microwave), you'll have to pay 72p. Well, I knew that electricity was expensive in Brutland, but I never imagined it was that expensive!

※

There is a strange Greek concept, represented by a strange Greek word: φιλότιμο. Its etymology combines the words for "love" and "honor". What it stands for, though, within the framework of that specific culture, is much more important: it represents a code of honour, a rectitude, that even villains are compelled to observe. I will explain its usage with an example. Let us assume that somebody does something which directly benefits me when s/he was under no obligation to do so. As a result of this gratuitous act of benevolence towards me, I feel impelled to reciprocate when the opportunity first arises. One of the ways to translate it would be a sense of *mutuality* or *reci-*

procity. Another, looser, example would be that if I know a friend to be in dire straits, I wouldn't expect him to buy a drink for the "round"; I will buy drinks for him for as long as I know that he can't afford it.

Now, there is *pseudo-mutuality* and there is *genuine mutuality*. The only difference between the two is that the former is a state of *mind* whilst the latter is a state of *heart*. And, of course, we could draw an analogy between treating somebody as a *mental image* (a thing), or as an *emotional image* (a person): pseudo-mutuality is then associated with treating people as *things* and genuine mutuality is associated with treating people as *persons*. When friendship is governed by standard rules followed in commercial transactions it is hardly worth being called such. But what is friendship?

One more of those signifiers that have betrayed their signifieds.

"Suffering is Good for the Soul"

An Englishman, even if he is alone, forms an orderly queue of one.

—**George Mikes**, *How to be an Alien*, p. 48

Queuing is the national passion of an otherwise dispassionate race.

—*ibid., p. 48*

"A native without his queue is a half-native", proverbially observed the Martian bruto-anthropologist Dr Silentiarius, and indeed, in many instances my personal observations have amply demonstrated the validity of the above statement. It is characteristic of the natives that, given the choice of a fast, warm, dry, indoors, non-queue cash withdrawal and a slow, freezing-cold, wet, outdoors, queue withdrawal, the overwhelming majority of them would give preference to the latter.

According to a psychological explanation propounded by the Neo-Freudian school of Psychoanalysis, we are dealing here with an instance of *masochism*, a symptom of the *Warm Uterus Phobic Syndrome* (WUPS!), under whose influence a quick entrance into something warm might trigger a *Temporary Vegetative State* (TVS).

> Deploring change is the unchangeable habit of an Englishman.
> —**Raymond Postgate**

Another instance of native masochism blatantly manifesting itself is the high-and-low temperature segregation that is religiously followed even in some of the most non-racist and progressive households. This apartheid in water temperature eternalizes itself by means of the *separate taps system*, according to which a combination of the two extreme, unfriendly-to-life temperatures is a non-option unless one decides to insert an aesthetically criminal bifurcate plastic tube appendage called a *mixer*.

The natives seem to have a very intimate and personal relationship with their Queen. They are constantly privy to her whereabouts, her personal life, her numerous sorrows and responsibilities. What is most notable, though, is that the Queen caters *in propria persona* to the natives, especially to those who have the habit of carbonising thinly chopped tobacco leaves and inhaling their toxic gasses.

The tobacco leaves, you see, are always supplied *by appointment to Her Majesty the Queen*.

Concord of Sweet Sounds?

The man that hath no music in himself,
Nor is not moved with concord of sweet sounds,
Is fit for treasons, stratagems, and spoils.
The motions of his spirit are dull as night,
And his affections dark as Erebus.
Let no such man be trusted.

—William Shakespeare, *The Merchant of Venice*, act V, sc. i,
(Lorenzo responding to Jessica's remark,
"I am never merry when I hear sweet music")

The English may not like music but they absolutely love the noise it makes.

—Sir Thomas Beecham, *A Mingled Chime*

There is no future for a musician in England no matter how serious he is; the English are philistines.

—Edward Elgar *in Elgar's tenth muse*, 12/5/1996 at 21:00, Channel Four

I have taste, after all, which is why I'm considered out of step with anything that could be regarded as slightly hip. And because I have taste, I don't really blend in with the general colour of 1987, people think I'm some kind of monument from the last century.

—**Morrissey** in **John Robertson**, *Morrissey In His Own Words*, p. 28

And this was the second movement of Beethoven's 7th symphony by... er... Beethoven.

—**Classic FM radio announcer**

The reason why Britain has produced so much innovative music is that if you come from a crappy nowhere town (and most of the best music does) you have to create something to compensate for the lack of anything going on. The key to Britain's musical prowess is boredom. Music is probably the biggest area in which we piss on the competition, but in the world of art, books and design I think we're ahead too. Pity about the food.

—**Jarvis Cocker**, *GQ*, December 1996, p. 187

> It had got to the point in music where people were really
> afraid to show how they felt; to show their emotions. I
> thought that was a shame, and very boring.
>
> —**Morrissey** in **John Robertson**, *Morrissey In His Own Words*, p. 28

The following is an excerpt from Dr Silentiarius' extant diaries
in which one witnesses a raw, sentimental (and unfortunately
utterly devoid of adequate scientific detachment) description of
the state of affairs in Brutland. However, I would like to be lenient
with him: anthropologists are not scientists in the strictest sense
of the word, but creatures resembling the tribe of hermaphro-
dites; in other words, they are a cross-breed, poets crossed with
scientists, and their field work amongst primitive peoples is highly
conducive to making them forget the idiom of science:

> Life without a decent classical music station
> Life with Classic FM and seldom apparitions of Chopin
> Descanting about congestion and that MI5 destination
> That is no destination of mine, having a piano but not a car
> And as loud timpani and vociferous tubas
> My concentration abuse
> J'accuse: life with Classic FM—*quel cauchemar*!

Why do so often I have the feeling that Classic FM is such *crap*
(to use this native slang term)? Because it reflects the dominant
ideology of all media, the ideology of consumerism, the ideology of people that sell addressing themselves to people that
buy. The deepest structure of the dominant ideology, though,
finds its expression in: *people without sensitivity addressing themselves to other people without sensitivity.* My "Classic FM" would
include non-classical (in strict terms) music and would exclude
noisy, bombastic, shallow classical music—especially after midnight, you vandals! My "Classic FM" would be called "Sensitivity
FM". It would neither sell nor buy—*it would share...*

I should have known better: only in Onanistan could one have
a classical music station in which, during the news, you hear the

voice of a football commentator screaming the description of a goal like a brute devouring his freshly snatched prey.

꿴

Much English music has the insipid flavour of the BBC Variety Orchestra playing an arrangement of a nursery tune.

—**Colin Wilson**, *Brandy of the Damned*

The Classic FM jingle—at its worst when sung by a raving coloratura. It works as a constant reminder of the fact that you shouldn't expect to hear anything "new" from this station as if, had there been such a case, you would have to take aspirins, paracetamols or anti-depressants in order to cope with the "shock of the new". Also, most of the stuff you'll hear will be on a Major scale—perhaps as a tribute to gay conservatism.

The only chance of hearing half-decent, half-unclichéd, non-ingratiating, minor-scaled, *deeper* classical music performed on classic FM is through the accidental death of a member of the royal family.

꿴

Indeed, the musical politics of Classic FM are indicative of a repressive state in a condition of red alert: *Defendemos la allegria* ("Let's defend joy"), reads Castro's graffito in a country where $15 is the standard monthly income. It is with this pretence towards gaiety—a bombastic, shallow, all-too-unconvincing gaiety—that the psychologically terminally ill citizens are exhorted. Funnily enough, in Cuba, despite the extreme poverty, people do manage to have a great time partying in the streets, dancing in the balconies, without discos, bars, expensive clothing, booze and drugs and all the other fixtures of the "civilized" and opulent West.

How do they do that?

Simply by not keeping themselves to themselves, by rejoicing in literal *con-viviality.*

The classic sonata brought to you this evening by Mercedes Benz.

—**Classic FM**

No, this station should not be named Classic FM, but *Mercedes Benz FM.* You see, in England, German cars are not really cars, but classical musicians and even, at certain times of the day, sonata deliverers. Do you want yours with pepperoni? How about Beethoven's appassionata with plenty of cheddar cheese on top?

The following was the description of a the contents of a CD by Hallmark entitled "The World of music—Greece":

Yannis Papadakis and Paraskevas Grekis bring the excitement of Greek music as played by their orchestra of bouzoukis and syrtakis.

Although the former—bouzouki—is an instrument, the latter—syrtaki—is a dance—something that obviously was beyond the knowledge of the writer.

Go anywhere in England where there are natural, wholesome, contented, and really nice English people; and what do you find? That the stables are the real centre of the household; and that if any visitor wants to play the piano the whole room has to be upset before it can be opened, there are so many things piled on it.

—**George Bernard Shaw**, *Heartbreak House, Act III*, Lady Utterword

I was in my room playing the piano when some noises coming from the living room next door distracted me. It was my housemates throwing cushions at each other, giggling, and making various other infantile noises.

Eventually I stopped playing. I went to the living room. "Some strange noises come from this room", I said in a joking manner. "Some strange noises come from that room", was the reply, as one of my housemates pointed in the direction of my room, still giggling.

I had been playing Chopin.

THAT, HOWEVER,

which offends even in the humanest Englishman, is his lack of music, to speak figuratively (and also literally): he has neither rhythm nor dance in the movements of his soul and body; indeed, not even the desire for rhythm and dance, for "music". Listen to him speaking; look at the most beautiful Englishwoman *walking*—in no country on earth are there more beautiful doves and swans; finally, listen to them singing! But I ask too much...

—**Friedrich Nietzsche**, *Beyond Good and Evil, in Oscar Levy (ed), The Complete Nietzsche, p. 210*

An Englishman's Home...

The lust for comfort murders the passion of the soul,
and then walks grinning in the funeral...
Your house shall not be an anchor but a mast.

—**Khalil Gibran**, *The Prophet*

HECTOR. We have been too long here. We do not live in
this house: we haunt it.

—**George Bernard Shaw**, *Heartbreak House*, Act III

Nation of shopkeepers? No, a nation of housekeepers, fretting and vacuum-cleaning and titivating our way to oblivion.

—**Michael Bywater**, *An Englishman's home is his prison,*
The Independent, 23/3/997

One day he [Dudjom Rinpoche] was driving through France with his wife, admiring the countryside as they went along. They passed a long cemetery, which had been freshly painted and decorated with flowers. Dudjom Rinpoche's wife said, "Rinpoche, look how everything in the West is so neat and clean. Even the places where they keep corpses are spotless. In the East not even the houses that people live in are anything like as clean as this".

"Ah, yes", he replied, "that's true; this is such a civilized country. They have such marvellous houses for dead corpses. But haven't you noticed? They have such wonderful houses for the living corpses too".

—**Sogyal Rinpoche**, *The Tibetan Book of Living and Dying*, p. 17

*T*here is at least one thing in Brutland, however, that indicates the possession of a miraculous degree of sensitivity. And this could be nothing else but their houses.

They do come in a wide variety, be they *terraced, detached,* or *semi-detached,* and (apart from the fact that they are usually one of the translator's worst nightmares) their surfaces (floors or, even worse, staircases) produce, in a quite docile manner, a wide variety of welcoming sounds upon contact with their residents' or, in exceptional circumstances, visitors' footsteps.

It is said that, due to this hyper-sensitivity, the natives often prefer to live on their own and have no visitors whatsoever, exclusively satisfying their modest need for companionship with domesticated felines. Those creatures seem to be the only ones capable of being trained to a discreet and noiseless pace: they are, as the natives say, the only animate beings that can be *house-trained.*

The disgusting squalor in which much of middle-class England lives has to be seen to be believed....

As a small child I was often physically overwhelmed by the nauseating dogginess of many respectable houses, where every chair stank of foetid wet retriever, where the scullery reeked of decomposing garbage and of gumboots covered in animal excrement, where every plate was cleaned by the cat's tongue though not much else, every surface thick with dust.

It is perhaps hardly surprising that we, the filthy English, are drifting into international obscurity on an ebb tide of bric-a-brac and cat lit.

—*Sunday Telegraph,* 25/8/1996

Spiros Doikas at a cemetery near Owens Park, Manchester, 1995

How do the natives wash their plates? Firstly they apply detergent to wet plates, which they allow to dry *without* rinsing the detergent off. Once I asked some students why they did that, as, in my opinion, it created a bit of a health hazard, "Well", came the retort, "if it [the detergent] was dangerous, they wouldn't sell it!"

૨&

If it were not for your guests all houses would be graves.

—**Khalil Gibran**, *Sand and Foam*

Sunday in Brutland: more than on any other day of the week, every house on the street becomes a silent, cloistered monument to itself. You need only take a short walk to be struck by the lack of commotion—the only exceptions being shopping areas (during shopping hours) and drinking areas (during drinking hours). Residential areas would be doomed to a perennial standstill if it were not for the occasional drunkard and the professional burglar. An evening stroll cannot but lead one to the conclusion that the inhabitants of this country are doomed to some sort of self-inflicted incarceration, imprisoned behind their century-old red brick walls and the ever-present, ever-tacky, lacy white curtains.

On weekdays the streets in residential areas are dead; on Sundays they are not only dead, but dead and buried. Hence it is easier to detect a walking cemetery than an aimless peripatetic. Only cemeteries are alive and kicking—with a fossilized romanticism, that is.

And every day is like Sunday.

Bloody Sunday.

Dr Silentiarius on houses:

> In Onanistan social life revolves on an exclusive basis
> around two houses: the *goggle house* and the *public house*.
> The sunny interval between them is called *rain*. Activities
> undertaken in either of these establishments seem always
> to make a very high demand on one's intellectual, emo-
> tional, and spiritual resources.
>
> However, some people are so exhausted after these
> activities that when driving back to the goggle house from
> the public house, and before they have the opportunity to
> devote themselves once more to a post-public house gog-
> glebox session, they have what they call *accidents*. Those
> that do survive (or merely avoid) these unfortunate and
> wanton occurrences feel obliged to devote themselves to
> another gogglebox session first thing in the morning, just
> in order to keep their gods happy.
>
> To conclude, I find this a versatile and wholly ntegrated
> spiritual approach to life.

Watching the Box Tonight... or, Alternative Spiritual Approaches

There is a profound and subliminal ideology that unites all—and that ideology is the ideology of consumerism. Some people ideologically place themselves as fascists, some others support an anti-fascist ideology, but both of them, beyond their respective ideologies, have something in common—and that is the ideology of consumerism. Consumerism is what I consider the real neo-fascism. Now that I am able to draw comparisons, I understand something that would shock many, something that would even shock me ten years ago: the fact that neither poverty nor exploitation are the worst of evils. That is to say, man's greatest evil is neither poverty, nor exploitation but the loss of human individuality under the state of consumerism. Under a fascist regime one could go to jail. But now, going to jail is of no use whatsoever. Fascism propped itself up on the shoulders of Church and Army, which appear insignificant in comparison to television.

—**Pier Paolo Pasolini**, in: Luis Racionero, *Las Filosofias Del Underground*, p. 63

So why do people keep on watching? The answer, by now, should be perfectly obvious: we love television because television brings us a world in which television does not exist. In fact, deep in their hearts, this is what the spuds crave most: a rich, new, participatory life.

—**Barbara Ehrenreich** ,"Spudding Out", in *The Worst Years of Our Lives*

So by all means let's have a television show quick and long, even if the commercial has to be delivered by a man in a white coat with a stethoscope hanging around his neck, selling ergot pills. After all the public is entitled to what it wants, isn't it? The Romans knew that and even they lasted four hundred years after they started to putrefy.

—**Raymond Chandler**, Letter, 15/11/1951
(published in *Raymond Chandler Speaking*, 1962)

Television is of great educational value. It teaches you while still young how to (a) kill, (b) rob, (c) embezzle, (d) shoot, (e) poison, and, generally speaking, (f) how to grow up into a Wild West outlaw or gangster by the time you leave school.

—**George Mikes**, *How to Be an Alien*

*would like to quote the extant remains of a poem from a famous native poet:

T. S. Helot, *The Love Song of J. Alfred Gogglebox*

Cras amet qui nunquam amavit,
quique amavit cras amet.

[May loveless love tomorrow, and may lover, too,
tomorrow find love.]
Anon, *Pervigilium Veneris*

Let us go then you and I
When the evening spreads out
Like a potato etherized upon a couch
Hence, in etherization, may commence holy communion
with the Couch Potato Union.

In the room women talk about Home and Away
Terry Christian, Chris Evans—with no dismay
No! I'm not Prince Charles,
nor was I meant to be;
and I won't have a big wedding on TV.
I'm just an attendant horde, whose vision
Is espoused to the television.

In the room women talk about Brookside
Pamela Anderson, Take That—joking aside

I have measured out my life with visions of the telly
precious sights of pneumatic bliss
gazes in inter-embracement,
aphiloprogenitive
and opticopro-
philiac.

...

In the room women talk about Top of The Pops
Neighbours, Cantona—chewing on their lollipops

Do I dare eat a leech? Do I dare suck a nipple?
I shall wear the tackiest union jack trousers
and jerk off upon a ripple.

I have seen the *koine* fornicating in the showers:
I do not think that they will take more than a tickle.

...

We have lingered by the chambers of the screen
By screen-girls wreathed with screen-weed red and brown
'Till human voices wake us, and we frown.

In his lonely isolation, Morris turned instinctively for sol-
ace to the media.

—**David Lodge**, *Changing Places*, p. 69

The above poem encapsulates the spiritual and transcendental essence of this alternative religion that imposes on its subjects such a demanding lifestyle. Few its followers, but inevitably *pulchrum est paucorum hominum* and that is that. But I will talk to you a bit about them.

Opticoprophiles, or *coggas* (conscientious gogglebox appendages), as they prefer to call themselves, share the common belief that the more vicariously one lives one's life, the more virtuous and fruitful that life will be. They also believe that one can achieve an unbounded awareness of the cosmos, the so-called *cosmic consciousness*, provided one spends a few decades of diligent daily meditation using the word *Brookside* as a mantra. "Oh God, give a man his daily Brookside/ so that he may learn to live aside" is one of their most oft-repeated prayers.

An extreme sect of this religion who called themselves *Hare Brookshna* would go about in the streets chanting this prayer, beating a drum and trying to proselytize others. But all their efforts were in vain: all prospective converts were at home, ...watching television.

≥®

Let us all now with one voice and one heart chant the holy song of the *coggas*:

> GOD, TAKE AWAY OUR LEGS, OUR HANDS, OUR VISION
> BUT DO NOT DEPRIVE US OF OUR TELEVISION!
> FOR IN OUR BRAIN'S BRAVE NEW LAND
> WE SEE PLENTY OF SPACE FOR A TELLY'MPLANT!

≥®

> For those of us finding Christmas just a teensy bit stress-ful, Santa had thoughtfully provided a spot of last-minute couch therapy.
>
> —*The Times*, 23/12/1996, Matthew Bond

Of course, one should not ignore the therapeutic value of television. It would not be an exaggeration to call it a medicine box for every known psychosomatic disorder, an emergency couch potato therapy easily administered without further social disruption. To quote the advice a native once gave a foreign girl for moments of depression, "You know... watch some crappy TV". Indeed, what a piece of advice:

> A note of caution here: Some distractors in themselves can perpetuate depression. Studies of heavy TV watchers have found that, after watching TV, they are generally more depressed than before they started!
>
> —**Daniel Goleman**, *Emotional Intelligence*, p. 73

It happened when I was sharing a flat with 4 other natives. One of them, Harry, I had never seen angry or heard swearing—that is until he realised that he couldn't find the "remote". Indeed, losing the remote control ranks as one of the major domestic disasters alongside burning a defrosted McCain pepperoni pizza or "cooking" a panful of water to extinction, leaving a rather unpleasant smell of burnt metal...

And it was only the video remote control; imagine what would have happened if it was the TV remote!

As

After numerous infertile cerebrations I feel that I am moving towards a gnosiological breakthrough. I think I have discovered serious clues on where the tortured, flagellated, deviated, stultified, etiolated, rummaged, eviscerated, repressed emotions of the natives have gone—in other words, I can give you the exact *longitude* and *latitude* (or should I say *pixel*) of their likely location:

> Television thrives on unreason, and unreason thrives on television. It strikes at the emotions rather than the intellect.
>
> —**Sir Robin Day**, *Financial Times*, 8/11/1989

Jai Guru Deva Om

In the East—though you might find this rather strange—there is no association of religion with gloom. In England, in the past at least, there was certainly a tendency to associate religion with gloom. People thought that the more serious and solemn and sad you looked, the more religious you were. If you went around happy and joyful, especially on the Sabbath, you were clearly an irreligious, impious, pagan sort of person. This may be an exaggeration, but I have heard that in the old days in Scotland you could be prosecuted for laughing on the Sabbath.

Unfortunately, Buddhism in Britain has also been affected by these attitudes, especially in the past. I remember that the first time I attended a Wesak celebration in London I was appalled. People looked as though they had come to a funeral—probably their parents'! When in the course of the talk I made a few jokes and humorous references some of the audience looked quite startled. A few did venture to smile and even to laugh, but it was clear that they were not accustomed to that sort of thing.

—**Sangharakshita**, *Vision and Transformation*, pp. 51-2

An Englishman thinks he is moral when he is only uncomfortable.

—**George Bernard Shaw**, *Man and Superman*, *"The Revolutionist's Handbook"*

The Society for the Suppression of Vice, founded in 1802, tried to stop people having fun at the fair.

—**Cosmo Landesman**,"May we have the pleasure?",
The Guardian, 17/10/1998

Almost every aspect of her religious faith, and practice (or the absence of it), is marked by contradiction and incoherence. (...)

Georgina [Britain], I am sad to say, has a poor appreciation of what underpins values of any kind, let alone "traditional values".

—**John Cornwell**,"Holy War", *The Sunday Times Magazine*, 21/7/1996, pp. 38-9

$\mathcal{N}$ative identity is consolidated only through the acquirement of *credentials*. *Credentialism* is a disease specifically linked to personal identity. And, of course, every name can be made more attractive than it really is with the appropriate series of arcane initials added immediately after it. The belief might even arise that every *person* can be made more attractive than (s)he really is by the same means. It is like the advertisement for the refined alcoholic drink: the advert maintains that the product in question is only available to beautiful people; similarly, credentials are only possessed by successful, *happy* people.

It is interesting that credentials are not limited to worldly affairs only. Spiritual credentials, for example, can be an authentic proof of spirituality. I will use an example to illustrate the disastrous effect of the lack of appropriate credentials for spiritual achievement.

The story (as told by Clive Sherlock in a lecture at the Manchester University Buddhist Society) is about somebody who rings the London Buddhist Society to announce that:

— I have just been enlightened!
— Well, what do you want us to do then?
— But don't you have a register or something?
— No sir, I'm afraid not.

The above demonstrates the existence of an unfortunate gap on the spirituality credentials side of things. On the other hand, enlightenment is not as yet fully accredited, as there is no such thing as a Doctor of Enlightenment (so to speak)—but perhaps somebody should make one up and rescue many a poor man from their misery.

❧

Transcendental Meditation (TM) is a paradigm of the "Heinz Beans" approach to spirituality. It is tinned, easy to use, and consumable within seconds; it has a long expiry date and can be bought easily (although one should note here that TM cannot yet be bought from a supermarket—but it could be bought through a newspaper containing a separate advertising leaflet).

The "Heinz Beans" approach implies the consumer's unwillingness to find the real thing in its pure, unprocessed state and cook it in an individual manner. TM has usurped a tradition of thousands of years, simplified it, done away with any notion of morality (businessmen and politicians have been known to practice it), extracted one of the active ingredients and sold it in a vitamin pack: twice a day before meals. (In that respect, it is reminiscent of DMT, the so-called "businessman's trip").

Moreover, the fact that canned spirituality has a price can only indicate one thing: that it is not spirituality. Real spirituality is invaluable, it has no price and it cannot be bought. What is real spirituality? Real spirituality is the *ressentiment* that every encounter with a being is something sacred. Something like believing that:

> All real living is meeting... where there is no sharing,
> there is no reality
>
> —**Martin Buber**, *I and Thou*

≈≈

> Georgina [Britain] is constantly prey to trendy notions. I have lost count of the various new-age sects she has enthusiastically advocated during RE lessons. (...)
>
> Her flightiness typifies the consumerist society, which dominates the lifestyle of the whole of her year. It strikes me that when she is in her new-age mood she is merely shopping around the proliferating do-it-yourself-help fads on offer.
>
> —**John Cornwell**, "Holy War", *The Sunday Times Magazine*, 21/7/1996, p. 39

> Wisdom ceases to be wisdom when it becomes too
> proud to weep, too grave to laugh, and too self-ful to
> seek other than itself.
>
> —**Khalil Gibran**, *Sand and Foam*

The New Age fad, although apparently a move in a good direction, is nothing really but a commercialization of spirituality, adopting the guise of its lighter, more digestible facets, a sort of "beam-me-up-Scotty" mysticism. "*Spiritual materialism*", a term (in effect an oxymoron) introduced by Chögyam Trungpa, is in fact the best way to describe this state of affairs.

On the other hand, the problem with those who do attempt to have a genuine spiritual life is that, no matter how well they practice ethics, prayer or meditation, their life, let alone their spiritual life, is too serious in the wrong way, too uptight, too self-ful and insular, in other words *it lacks vitality*—and if we go to the root of this word then we realise that a spiritual *life* without *vitality* is a spiritual void.

The equivalent of the Martian Bible is called *Argos brochure*. Indeed, I deduced that after a conversation I had with a couple of Indians. They informed me that their religious book is called *Bhagavad-Gita* and can be found in every home in India. Similarly, they continued, you can find the Argos brochure in every English home. And my very logical syllogism was that since you can find this book in every native home it should be their religious manual! I believe that native masters of logic, renowned worldwide for their scientific integrity, will congratulate me in due time for the impeccability of my reasoning.

TM is not bad (and DMT is contained in the human organism). It is a good thing to do especially if you're SAD—that is to say, if you're suffering from *Seasonal Affective Disorder*, or even *Lifelong Affective Disorder*. In other words, it's good if you're a SAD LAD, that is to say someone who bears the burden of *Lifelong Affective Disorder* with a certain degree of quiet desperation but who fails to cope with the occasional seasonal outbreaks.

However, it should be borne in mind that spiritual goods do have a price, along with everything else in this world. I hope that I didn't surprise you! Money, you know, can greatly expand your world consciousness! Gotcha! You didn't know that either, did-jah? And the price of this spiritual good is roughly equivalent to the average street price of 10 grams of coke, or just 6 grams of coke if you're a student. Or tuppence a day for the next 60 years of your life—40 if you're a student. At a price like that it's a snip, isn't it?

We have seen how spirituality, in its divine form, is associated with pints. Yet, spirituality, also in its cultural form, is the same way inclined. In order to tolerate the rather unconventional language of poetry the natives have decided to serve it with pints; it is like making a very deep movie about the human condition but adding deliberately a few titillating sex scenes, in order to make it more palatable. Poetry with pints then:

> THE NEWTON BREWERY INN
> WEBBS LANE, MIDDLEWICH
> PRESENTS
> POETRY WITH PINTS
> THE SECOND WEDNESDAY IN EVERY MONTH
> 8-30 PM
> A PLETHORA OF POETRY
> AND ALL MANNER OF MUSIC
> FROM CHESHIRE'S PERFORMANCE POETS
> AND MUSICIANS

POETS, STORYTELLERS, SINGERS & MUSICIANS
ALL WELCOME OR JUST COME ALONG AND LISTEN

My humble opinion is that Blake's poetry has gravely influenced this attitude:

> The road of excess leads to the palace of wisdom.
> Prudence is a rich ugly old maid courted by Incapacity.
>
> —William Blake, *The Marriage of Heaven and Hell*

The Brits, masters as they are in poetry and the other fine arts, and far from being "old maids", have instinctively internalized this sacred insight. The natives who do not partake of this wisdom, are a shame to their very own race.

And talking of pubs and poetry, we should not exclude prose from similar schemes. The so-called "literary pub crawls" have become fashionable all over the country, starting with Dublin. If you do take one yourself you'll see with your own eyes the places famous writers frequented in order to find inspiration in the exalted atmosphere of refined spirits. Some brewers noted the fact that a great part of their most loyal clientele were men of higher intelligence, and named their beers accordingly. For example, a Cardiff brewery called its bitter "Brains".

Funnily enough, not only spirituality has the prerogative of being associated with pints. *Spiritualism*, too. I had been to the first meeting of the first spiritualist society in the country to be funded by a university. I had enrolled in this society (as well as others) during *Freshers' Week* as part of my research into current trends that are popular with the natives. Naturally, I was invited to their first meeting. I consider myself a hero for having managed to put up for a whole hour with a shamefully patronizing charlatan who credited himself with psychic abilities. There was meant to be a break. Ten minutes afterwards, when the "parish" reassembled, I noticed a small difference: the founders of the society and the *soi-disant* medium had brought with them their lovely pints. Spirits must have found that very exciting. I don't know whether a plethora of them appeared in the second half—if they did, I missed them.

❧

It seems that a primary requirement for the cultivation of friendly feelings towards others is the ability to be *mindful* of their existence, to be *aware* of the space they occupy, their physiognomies, their expression, their body language. And it is precisely a lack of awareness, a lack of *appreciative attention* towards others that is lacking in the Brutish. It seems, moreover, that the outside environment is paid the same lip service as the inner, emotional environment.

But even before we get to the stage of cultivating friendly feelings towards others we have to be able to cultivate friendly feelings towards ourselves—and it is in this that the whole of Western Civilization, let alone Brutish culture, is deficient. And by "friendly feelings" I do not mean egoism or self-conceit or anything of the sort, but a peaceful acceptance of ourselves as virtuous, guiltless beings in peaceful and harmonious co-existence with our inner selves. In other words, *charity begins at home.*

I remember attending a meditation class in FWBO's *Manchester Buddhist Centre* where *metta bhavana* (meditation on loving-kindness) was practiced. After the end of the session, a perfectly amiable old man brought up this problem: he found it difficult to develop friendly feelings towards himself; he didn't "like himself", he said. The meditation instructor was at a loss for a remedy and starting beating about the bush.

Indeed, *metta bhavana* is one of the ideal practices for the Brutish disease of self-dislike and inability to adopt behavioural patterns of friendliness and openness. Now, how to cope with the problem illustrated in the meditation example above? Sometimes only a community embodying *metta* (rather than expatiating on it) can really be a living proof of its feasibility to somebody who, say, has never believed in colours. Indeed, how do you talk to the blind about colours? Maybe synaesthetically, for example through hearing the joyful cries of a baby who is playing with the reflections of a swirling prism on a sunny day...

What is professor Silentiarius' conclusion regarding the spiritual side of things in *Old Blighty*?

> People in Onanistan share a great deal of noble values relating to family, personal integrity, relationships, hospitality, spirituality and a number of other areas that will not be named for the sake of brevity and clarity of expression although they could be succinctly summarized with one word which encapsulates, to a great extent, the essence of them all: *money*.

Hours of Darkness

Hours of darkness
Sun rises: 7.46 am
Sun sets: 3.54 pm
Moon sets: 11.18 am
Moon rises: 12.09 pm

—*The Times*, December 2 1996

The inhabitants of Britain are said to be sprung from the soil and to preserve a primitive lifestyle...They are simple in their habits and far removed from the cunning and knavishness of modern man. Their diet is inexpensive and quite different from the luxury that is born of wealth. The island is thickly populated, and has an extremely chilly climate, as one would expect in a sub-Arctic region.

—**Pytheas**, Greek geographer (325-285 BC)

"I thought perhaps it always rained or looked dark in England". Mary said.
"Eh! no!" said Martha, sitting up on her heels among her black lead brushes. "Nowt o'th'soart".

—**Frances Hodgson Burnett**, *The Secret Garden*, p. 60

Rain is one of the principal products of England.
—**Peter Cagney**, *The Book of Wit and Humour*, 2596

I don't desire to change anything in England except the weather.
—**Oscar Wilde**, *The Picture of Dorian Gray*

Whenever people talk to me about the weather, I always feel certain that they mean something else.
—**Oscar Wilde**, *The Importance of Being Earnest*

I like the weather,—when it is not rainy,
That is, I like two months of every year.

—**Byron,** *Beppo, XLVIII*

An inevitable part of the natives' everyday life, throughout the
ten-month-long local winter, is their habit of releasing *mucus*
from their upper respiratory passage into their environment, and
more specifically, through gentlemen's handkerchiefs (applicable
to both sexes), tissues, serviettes or, as the case may be, *bog-
roll*—this for those lacking in the appropriate degree of sophis-
tication. Eventually all Brutlanders find themselves afflicted by
this unavoidable seasonal occurrence that cannot yet, by any scientific method hitherto devised, be counteracted.

The above observation leads me naturally to the spontaneous cogitation that the name "Brutland", apart from being too
harsh, does not reflect a very important quality of this country. A considerable improvement would do a great service to
realistic verisimilitude and would make the prose writers of the
future eternally thankful:

What about "Cloud*mucu*land"?

☙

When two Englishmen meet, their first talk is of the weather.

—**Samuel Johnson,** *The Idler, No 11*

Many original and extremely witty things have been said about
the native habit of commenting on the weather. What my observations have verified is the fact that this subject offers itself as
the ideal access to conversation without the unnecessary side-
effect of communication. Indeed, it is *cool* to talk about the
weather; especially if it is rainy. Tell me, in which other country could you have the expression "as right as rain" to denote
something which is perfectly all right?

> The Englishman is no missionary, no conqueror... He carries the English weather in his heart wherever he goes, and it becomes a cool spot in the desert and a steady and sane oracle amongst all the deliriums of mankind.
>
> —**George Santayana**, *Soliloquies in England* (1922)

> The climate of England has been the world's most powerful colonizing impulse.
>
> —**Russell Green**

How do the English cope with the English weather? It is simple: simply by being *unimpassioned*; in other words—*by being English*. The long, lulling, unending drizzle, the overdarkened skies, the nominal existence of seasons are all part of a living metaphor of something that doesn't vibrate anymore, something that has undergone an *inner death*. In the English weather I can see the ultimate reflection of Englishness; in the English countenance I can see the ultimate expression of the English weather.

When the English ventured abroad with imperial intent, was it by any chance because they were trying to rid themselves of the effects the weather had had on them as it seeped through their collective unconscious, imbuing them with undesirable character traits? Was it in fact an innovative form of behavioural pattern reorganisation?

I plead ignorance; ask the Indians.

Strange Customs

*A*mongst the natives, superstition, as I have mentioned before, and belief in arcane practices, were at one time rampant. A case in point: they thought they had found a vaccine for a new, disastrous epidemic that was spread through meat-cylinder insertion.

The vaccine was supposed to be worn pinned to their clothes in order to allow the slow release of active agents. Its physical appurtenances were those of a *red ribbon* and it was also known colloquially as the *AIDS ribbon*. And indeed, the individuals who adopted this simple, yet effective technique, seemed to develop an (unexplainable to laymen) immunity to the disease—not to mention an *avant-guard* fashion consciousness.

A different line of interpretation has it that the natives, in adopting this trendy practice, simply demonstrated a feeling of *condom fatigue*, that is to say the AIDS ribbon was the last word in *alternative condomization* and *venereal autocondomentation*.

❧

An invention bearing close affinity to the *Aids Prevention Device* (red ribbon), was the *Accident Prevention Device*, otherwise known as *Red Nose*. It was distributed by the authorities once a year as part of the *Comic Appeal* campaign.

This device, however, was not limited to its strictly protective function; it was also meant as a humour stimulant for Brutish vehicles. It is well known that the natives are so kind-hearted towards their cars because they don't want them to suffer the same lack of humour suffered by their drivers and passengers.

A similar yearly occurrence was the ritualistic wearing of a plastic poppy in one's upper garments, the so-called *Poppy Appeal*. It was done for the sacred memory, fiscal relief and possible resurrection of the patriotic co-natives who devoted themselves to pushing up poppies during the first world war.

Eventually, some of them still managed to accomplish their patriotic duty without an infantile rush to play with flowers. And a few of them have remained until today. Very few of them indeed.

It is evident from the above (*Red* Ribbon, *Red* Nose, *Red* Poppy) that the colour *Red* possessed a number of healing properties that extended from the prevention of sexually transmitted diseases and the prevention of accidents on motorways to the potentially resuscitative commemoration of those who died for the Land of Hope and Glory. Some people even thought of extracting its active ingredient and selling in to the masses— thus hoping to add some colour to their lives. Who knows, maybe in a few years' time we'll be able to buy it from our local health food shop.

One thing however, that is practically impossible to buy in Brutland is unadulterated surgical spirit (ethyl alcohol); you can only get it in a mixture with the denaturant *methanol* that makes it smell foul and taste even worse. I found this fact puzzling until I met a pharmacist who told me of the following incident which took place when she was working for a pharmaceutical company. She was vainly trying to find the lab's reserves of alcohol as it was necessary for some experiment. A colleague explained to her where it had all gone: "Suzy had a party last week and she used it for the punch". Now I can understand why a *denaturant* renders a substance unfit to eat or drink without destroying usefulness in other applications, and why such things as denaturants are needed: rather than queuing outside off-licenses to get their dose, natives would have queued outside pharmacies. And funnily enough, this sounds just about right.

One fairly reliable way of measuring the working classness of an area is by the density of *lollipop persons* (constable-free traffic regulators) per 1/4 of a square mile. Of course, measurements have to be taken during the hours when children go to school and come back from school. To be precise, density 0-2 per 1/4 of a square mile indicates an opulent neighbourhood; 2-6 a well-off neighbourhood; 6-10 a not so well-off neighbourhood; 6-10 is a close to breadline neighbourhood—and anything more than 10 should be considered a breadline neighbourhood.

Similarly, one can decide class by the supermarket used. Hence, people inhabiting in density 0-2 areas buy their food from Mark and Spencers; 2-6 from Tesco and Safeways; 6-10 mainly from

We've got treats for you!

Kwiksave and Aldi but sometimes also Tesco, and anything higher than 10 almost exclusively from Kwiksave and Aldi.

⁂

Book storing and retailing outlets (libraries and bookshops) offer a unique way for an educated observer to calculate how much time has passed since the erection of their premises. And I'm not talking about the carbon 14 method, which uses a naturally radioactive carbon isotope (with atomic mass 14 and a half-life of 5,780 years) to determine the age of the usual organic, geologic, or archaeological specimens of intergalactic civilizations.

No, there is a technologically inferior, yet quicker, method. I will explain myself. In Brutland one can judge the age of these edifices by measuring the amount of smegma which has accumulated on their computers. The method is similar to the one used for measuring the age of a tree, i.e., counting the rings in a section of the trunk. This is a foolproof method owing to the fact that, since their purchase, these apparatuses are never meant to undergo any polishing or dusting whatsoever—that is considered a waste of time.

⁂

Quoting from Dr Silentiarius's diary:

> An inexplicably large number of natives will be seen walking about with what I call *a chip on their buttocks*. This reminds me of the tribe which was the object of scrutiny in one of my previous expeditions, the Bushmen of Kalahari, who retain excess fat in their out-of-proportion buttocks as an energy repository for their long trips in the barren dessert. However, the Onanistan natives do exhibit a trait which I find peculiar to them—that is to say, one can easily recognise a tension in the back area as they walk. (This is lacking in the bushmen.)

At first I could find no reasonable explanation for this unsightly proctological protuberance, but an alternative medic in Brutland told me that it was due to a cultural defect called *anal retentiveness*. He added that in older times natives were so terrified of this disease (also called "constipation") that many cases suffering from it would be referred to Dr Arbuthnot Lane's knife. The good doctor would relieve them of their suffering by removing the noxious large intestine and giving them the blessing of chronic and irreversible diarrhoea.

It is regrettable that less drastic therapeutic regimes, such as high colonic irrigation, do not constitute an acceptable option; the retentive nature of the natives' anuses renders that therapy a yet unaccomplished breakthrough in hydrokinetic engineering.

On the other hand, perhaps as an extreme reaction to the general tendency towards *anal retentiveness*, I have sometimes witnessed the opposite, namely *anal looseness*. I drew my conclusions after carefully observing a certain area in a town called Redbrick. One of the most famous streets in that area, with plenty of trendy bars and cafes, is called *Canal Street*. Well, not exactly. The first letter of both words on the street sign had been well-nigh obliterated, thus making the sign allude to what I was told was one of the local community's favourite practices (*anal treet*, or, if we correct the misspelling: *anal treat*). Later I realised that anal looseness was related to affective preference minorities.

we should be careful
Of each other, we should be kind
While there is still time.
—**Philip Larkin**, *Collected poems*, p. 214

Far be it from me to censure the natives either for their pagan-
ism or for their belief in the underlying animate state of apparently inanimate entities. Indeed, how could I, when even the
doors in Brutland so urgently require of you such gentle, controlled behaviour, that, if otherwise treated, they release upon
you a vindictive wrath equal to that of bad-tempered Olympian
gods? Let this be the paramount lesson: never confuse the two
keywords that have two of three phonemes in common: *push*
and *pull*.

And it is even harder for the non-native speaker when the
push/pull dialectic is represented by two adjoining doors, the
first one with a "push" on it and the second one with a "pull",
as is the case in a number of public buildings. Well, it took me
three years to come to grips with the *push/pull* challenge without making a constant fool of myself; so if you have trouble
yourself in that area, take heart: you are not alone.

However, one should do one's outmost to be kind to doors in
Brutland: a *faux pas* can transform them from angels to demons.
They always demand some sort of attention, and not just for the
above-mentioned reason.

Some say that doors in Brutland insist upon closing themselves
due to fear of conflagration.

I explain myself: in AD 1666 the capital of Brutland, Big-Ben
City, was burned to cinders due to the negligence of archaic
doors, which had a limited consciousness development. That is
to say, if doors had had enough spiritual insight into the facts of
the world, they would have closed by themselves, thus drasti-
cally limiting the spread of the fire. This is one traumatic event
that marked the history of this land and stigmatised the hearts
of its denizens, who still bear a massive grudge against doors.

Since then, the natives have thoroughly trained their doors' consciousness to function on a higher moral and intellectual plain. Modern doors are developed to the extent of closing automatically—thus restricting the spread of fear. Indeed, I can understand the natives' pyrophobia, cognisant as I am (and having had first hand experience) of the uncontrolled pyromaniac tendencies of university students.

~

Not only humanoids, not only inanimate objects, but also representatives of the animal realm seem to take a highly original and subversive stance towards reality. I animadvert here to the local cockerels who, although they don't drive on the left side of the road like the humans, emit such audible signals as to startle and nonplus any wanderer of the Milky Way. Indeed, in the whole known universe cockerels produce a sound which is a variation on the theme of *kirikiki*; in Brutland, however, they shout out *cock-a-doodle-doo*!

~

What happens to students after they graduate? Well, they go to the Department of Social Security (DSS). Went to the DSS today myself in order to apply for unemployment benefit, or, as it has been renamed, "Jobseeker's Allowance" (JSA). Pity… at least the previous one had a form with what seemed like a musical annotation—UB 40 or "oobeh quarantah", as the Italians say.

So I took a numbered ticket and waited until it was time for my number to be called. After five minutes I felt myself verging on incontinence, so I thought, "I'd better find out where the gentlemen's facilities are around here". Indeed, the security staff was very helpful at that, and I proceeded to perform my biological need. However, as I opened the door, I couldn't help but notice a massive sign above the toilet reading:

PLEASE
DO NOT USE DRUGS
AS IT CAN BE DANGEROUS
TO CHILDREN

I mused to myself, "However big this sign is, if somebody is in a state in which he needs to use needles, then it won't make much difference". But still, I couldn't conceptualize the danger that was meant. What in hell, I'm in a civilized country, I thought.

Then I remembered an English guy I had met in Mexico who told me the following story. He was going to London by train when somebody sounded the alarm. A middle-aged woman was screaming blue murder. What had happened was that her daughter had been to the toilet, but had never come out of it. When the woman finally entered the toilet, she saw her daughter lying there with a needle stuck in her head!

Kurt was right, and of course this is the right context to remember him as well:

> Still, the reindeer went on reproducing. There were these useless, big black animals everywhere, and a lot of them had very bad dispositions. They were given small amounts of money every month, so they wouldn't have to steal. There was talk of giving them very cheap dope too—to keep them listless and cheerful, and uninterested in reproduction.
>
> —**Kurt Vonnegut**, *Breakfast of Champions*, p. 164

In Penny Lane...

In Penny Lane there is a barber showing photographs
Of every head he's had the pleasure to have known ...

—**The Beatles**, "Penny Lane"

*L*et us say you are visiting that barber and you have forgotten not the name of the street, but what *genus* of street it is—in this case a *Lane*. The implication of this may be that you will never get there unless you get more precise information. I will make myself clear forthwith: in Brutland you have a number of different signifiers for the signified "street" (that is to say, "a public way or thoroughfare in a city or town, usually with a sidewalk").

For example, we could have in the same town "Harley Street", "Harley Avenue", "Harley Crescent", etc. One would expect that there is some logic in the usage of such specialized terminology, a terminology that often makes the lives of Asian taxi drivers miserable. Of course, to a certain extent these different signifiers define the shape, size or surroundings of the public way or thoroughfare in question. Hence, one should expect an avenue to be a rather big street or broad roadway lined with trees; or, at least, (and this is chiefly British usage) "the drive leading from a main road up to a country house".

However, this is not always so. In Redbrick, for instance, there is a street called "Harley Avenue" which is about 50 metres long, has no trees, and does not lead to a country house, in fact it is just another boring street of terraced houses! And the list of "synonyms" is endless: *Alley, Approach, Arcade, Arch, Back, Bridge, Broadway, Buildings, Common, Court, Circle, Circus, Crescent,*

Drive, Gardens, Gate, Green, Grove, Hill, Lane, Little, Mews, Mount, Parade, Park, Passage, Path, Place, Promenade, Rise, Road, Street, Terrace, Walk, Way, Vale, View, Yard... The moral of the story is that you *always* have to remember what kind of public way or thoroughfare it is when setting off for somewhere; otherwise you might never get to see those damn photographs.

If we admit the complexities of street naming in Brutland, then what can we say about the way street crossings are encoded? It was when I was trying to rent a house and I had to ring the land-lord in order to take directions from him regarding the where-abouts of his property that I first encountered the apparently cryptic expression *pelican crossing*. My imagination had already been excited towards the zoological side of things, as I had already heard of another such expression, similar in linguistic formation but different in zoological specification: *zebra crossing*. In vain I kept looking for pelicans and zebras that were crossing the streets of Brutland. Human brutes were not only predomi-nant; they were the only ones.

Down the Wooden Hills to Petfordshire

Do you remember the first time?

—*A song by Pulp*

*I*t was Sunday when I arrived in Big-Ben city, capital of Brutland. Imagine, me, Spiros Doikas, at last a citizen of the world! And apart from the extremely scary reminder of Big Brother (*Mind the Gap!, Mind the Gap!, Mind the* [frigging] *Gap!...*) I managed to find my way around quite well, with the help of a bloke I met in the tube. Finally, there I was at my last stop, a station in the south suburbs of the city.

I had heard of that famous area before. It was where many people gathered yearly in order to twist their necks as they tracked the irregular trajectories of a small, yellow ball bandied to and fro over a fishing net—or that's what it looked like to a person like me who has always lived on an island and has had plenty of fishing experience. However, I never really managed to understand the paradox here that the one whose net catches the greatest amount of fish will be the loser. Erm... I beg your pardon, I meant balls actually. People would pay a lot of money in order to watch people who would be really good at not allowing their nets to catch balls, and the winners themselves would be deified and lavishly rewarded. "What a strange custom", I thought to myself.

Upon arrival at the station I was instructed to contact my prospective hostess by means of the telephone device. Immediately after my disembarkation I was lucky enough to find such a device readily available. I seemed, however, to have difficulty operating the machine, as it was rather capricious in its choice of coins. A young lady (with a violin on her back) was kind enough to choose the ones most likely to be accepted from the smorgasbord of coins that lay in my open, sweaty, palm.

At last, I could triumphantly declare my arrival! The phone rung twice. "Hello", a posh, squeaky voice sounded in the headphone. "It's me", I replied, "Spiros... I have arrived!" "Well", she shrilled, "stay exactly where you are". She hung up. "Exactly where I am", I thought to myself. "That's dead easy". I spent the next three hours in patient attendance whilst watching two teenage tube persons gallantly exchange pleasantries.

"Exactly where I was"—that was the key to my salvation, I thought; but "exactly where I was" meant next to the trains, inside the station, a fact that my dear hostess failed to conceptualize. As time grew heavy upon my shoulders and various doubts about my salvation proliferated and multiplied like Christians having intercourse, I deemed it wise to make another attempt at contacting her Divinity.

"*Where are you?*" she screamed in a soprano voice that had been castrated of all musicality. "*I've been to three stations with the name you gave me and couldn't find you, and the traffic, oh, my goodness, it was appalling!*" I had to explain this time in detail my location. "Oh, I am sorry, I didn't know that they had phones next to the platforms... Anyway, stay where you are, I'm coming to pick you up", she said once again before hanging up, sending cold shivers down my spine. Naturally, "stay where you are" had assumed by now rather unsavoury connotations. This time however, it worked, and after four hours of waiting, by which time the day had become night, I arrived safe and sound at the house.

She opened the door and I proceeded through the spacious living room that led to a very beautiful *conservatory* (I thought, "that's what must make all the difference between common and not-common people"). I was struck by two things. First, there was a portrait of the Queen, which immediately made me think of the Penny Lane fireman. "Aha", I thought, "this guy knows his Beatles". But the parallel was not exact. In the portrait there was not just Her Majesty alone: she was surrounded by a few dozens of men dressed in blue or grey suits who were smirking as if they were getting something nice done to their private parts. Amongst these men I noticed the man of the house. "Well" I thought, "I am honoured to share—albeit temporarily—lodgings with a man who has been immortalized in such close proximity to her Highness. This is something I will never forget".

The second thing that struck me was the absurd number of postcards that seemed to be wishing happy birthday to Jack, a *persona non existens* as far as I was concerned, and I thought I had some first-hand evidence for that. I knew, for example, that they had three daughters, Jane, Miriam and Natasha, and that the mother herself was called Mona. Moreover, no further members of the family could have possibly been procured: the last time I had seen my hostess, she had had a perfectly flat belly. And that was only five months ago.

The mystery of this situation immediately seized me. I felt like Hercules Poirot ready to dip into the unknown and reveal the truth in an amazing fit of mental acrobatics. I never let myself down, and I knew that this time, once again, I would not fail. You see, for some strange reason, I had confidence in myself or, at least, in the workings of destiny that leave nothing without an explanation for too long.

As I stood there on my own (my hostess had retired in order to receive a private phone call), I faintly heard some noises that could only be produced by a non-human animal. I didn't have to wait for long: there emerged a short-legged canine, with a bizarre tendency to have non-heterosexual sex with strangers that belonged to a hairy, similarly carbon-based, albeit bipedal species. "Poor thing, it has never been instructed in anatomical correctness", I thought.

"Jack, come here, darling. Up, up the wooden hills to Bedfordshire!", cracked the voice of my hostess in the offing, interrupting my premature cogitations on issues of some import.

୭ⅆ

> Though vociferous in her defence of animal "rights", she [Britain] is increasingly rude to humans.
>
> —**Lesley White**, "Riot Acts", *The Sunday Times Magazine*, 21/7/1996, p. 44

Apart from doors there is another kind of entity that demands great attention in Brutland. Domesticated animals, by dint of the fact that they lack that tool of obfuscation and misunderstanding we call "language", fulfil an amazing number of the natives' communicative exigencies.

A species of the feline family is so profoundly worshipped in Brutland that it is entitled to prerogatives not even humanoids could enjoy. Indeed, in this, Brutland reminded me of ancient Egypt, and a breeze of exoticism whisked through my heart. Felines have it so good that humanoid companies compete to produce the yummiest eating substances for them, and advertisements abound in the gogglebox that are addressed *directly* to the admirable creatures.

To show the extent of the worship that humanoids bestow on their pussies, I will have to mention that a *National Health System*, under the twinned aegis of the *National Cat Protection League* and the *National Canine Defence League*, has been engineered to cater to their needs:

> VETS in Manchester have launched Britain's first brain scanner for pets...

Some humanoid-friendly voices, though, have advocated that the scanner also be used for humanoid patients, notwithstanding the fact that they obviously originate from a lower caste:

> Pip Boydell... said he wants to make the scanner availa-
> ble for people if needed.

However, until this becomes standard practice certain humanoids will have to go without this feline-oriented facility:

> The hospital was unable to give a scan to 10-year-old
> Nicholas Geldard, who was then sent on a desper-
> ate search for treatment in other north-west hospitals
> before he died.
>
> —*Manchester Evening News*, 22/3/1996

Well, that's what happens to you in Brutland if you are not a cat.
But don't despair, nothing bad is devoid of something good: cats,
like wars, *assist tremendously the advance of science.*

> Angry Margaret Magee has divorced her husband John
> claiming he loved his DOG more than her. (...) She wrote
> on divorce papers: "I hope you and Ben will be very
> happy".
>
> A neighbour said: "We can understand why he thinks
> such a lot of Ben, he's a lovely dog. John is always with
> him. They are never apart. I can understand why he
> would prefer him to a woman. At least he won't get any
> ear-ache off Ben".
>
> Last night a legal expert said it was "highly unusual" for
> animals to be named in divorce petitions. He added: "It's
> much more common for another woman or man to be
> named, but I suppose if the aggrieved party feels the ani-
> mal is responsible then there is no reason why they can't
> be included too".
>
> —*Daily Star*, front page, 7/9/1996
> "TIL PET US DO PART- Divorce over dog"

However, one must not forget that there are ways to keep pets' social radicalism at bay. In our day and age, with computers and all, it is even easier. So only not even you can be sure that your husband will not run away with his favourite dog; you can, also, be sure that when you stroke your feline you stand no chance of getting scratched by its felonious nails:

> PEOPLE who are allergic to cats are being given the chance to pet and foster a kitten of their own. A new CD-ROM... introduces virtual reality cats as interactive computer pets.
>
> —*The Times*, 16/9/1996 (front page!)
> "Now pet lovers can stroke the cat sitting on their laptop"

As a part of my scientific investigation into the *one-night-stand phenomenon*, I decided to follow the steps that would probably lead me to experience said phenomenon. I went to a live music venue that night, in order to attend what the natives call a "gig". I saw a girl standing next to me, sipping what would be her fourth pint. I moved towards her, "You wouldn't have the time by any chance, would you?" I asked, to which she was keen to reply, "Yes, it is half past eleven". "Brilliant band", I added, "What do you reckon of them... I especially dig the bass player, really strong hands...".

And that was it. I managed to touch base on the solid basis of chit-chat. "Would you like to come home for a smoke?" she said when it was about ten to two. I was not sure at the time but later confirmed that this native euphemism referred to a bit more than ordinary tobacco or plain old-fashioned *shag*.

I was in for a surprise. It seems that her deviant feline was in the mood for a spot of three-in-a-bed action, and it hopped on the bed meowing in an "it's-not-fair-to-let-me-out-of-the-game" complaint. Unfortunately I couldn't do much about it as

I was too distracted by the already advanced intercorporeal activities in which I found myself engaged. It was only when the cat started rubbing itself against my lower thigh, while increasing the intensity and pitch of its meowing, that I was forced to some kind of erection, erm... reaction in order to save myself from the cat's raging jealousy (and the inopportune epiphenomenon of a bloody array of punctures on parts of my body alarmingly close to the holy of holies).

In the morning, when the experiment was over (probably for both of us), and after she had eaten a tangerine in bed without even thinking of offering some to me, she revealed the cat's *veritable raison d'être*: "I will not have children, so that's the closest I'll ever get to caring for somebody". I believe that VHEMT (Voluntary Human Extinction Movement) would have been pretty pleased with her.

If I can remember well, I met that lady the day after. Our ways crossed; she didn't even acknowledge my existence—after all she didn't really know me now, did she?

I was just someone she had sex with...

The Art of Amusing Oneself Sadly

Most mass entertainments are in the end what D.H. Lawrence described as "anti-life". They are full of a corrupt brightness, of improper appeals and moral evasions. To recall instances: they tend towards a view of the world in which progress is conceived as a seeking of material possessions, equality as a mere levelling, and freedom as the ground for endless irresponsible pleasure. These productions belong to a vicarious, spectators' world; they offer nothing which can really grip the brain or heart.

—**Richard Hoggart**, *The Uses of Literacy*, p. 340

Life like a permanent wank inside you.

—**Richard Hoggart**, *The Uses of Literacy*, p. 247

The English amuse themselves sadly according to the custom of their country.

—**Duc de Sully**, *Memoirs* (1630)

The English race is the best at weeping and the worst at laughing.
(Anglica gens est optima flens et pessima ridens.)

—**Thomas Hearne**, *Reliquiae Hearnianae*

Thank Gawd all this new year stuff is over for another 12 months. Miserable old goat I may be, but I cannot stand all the forced, cheery, gang piss up that is New Year's Eve. Why anyone wants to go to Trafalgar square to be crushed by a beery mob of semi-comatose drongoes who don't know each other, I cannot imagine.

—**Jo Brand**, *The Independent*, 4/1/1997

But in post-industrial, post-imperial Britain, enjoyment is important to our identity and self-esteem. In the absence of empire, economic prowess or grand political projects, what we like to do for fun defines who we are—a sense of patriotism based on pleasure. Yet when it comes to passions, Britain is a tribal society.

—**Cosmo Landesman**, "May we have the pleasure?",
The Guardian, 17/10/1998

Newcastle Brown: the drink of love.

—*Advert for Newcastle Brown Ale.*

Drink helped to reduce the inhibitions of courting couples, who found privacy and recreation in the drinking place... the drinking place was "neutral ground" in love as in business.

—**Brian Harrison**, *Drink and the Victorians*, p. 42

They gather together in dark, overcrowded venues (sometimes called *dives*) and miraculously manage to remain indifferently apart (A sentence from a romantic short-story by D.H. Lawrence springs to mind: "They stood together, apart".) To their personal adornment of military boots and many untacked layers of clothes they will add the accessory of a Liquid Yeast Extract receptacle, and sip it with slow, minimal, ritualistic movements. *There* is the epicentre of their *agapic* functions; *there* has their heart *transfused*.

It's like a big funeral in which everybody mourns himself *personally* and nobody acknowledges the existence of fellow-mourners. No big deal, as everybody is obliged to bury oneself—*daily*. Now, seated figures of docile somnambulists metamorphose into folded upright coffins (like the one you get in Magritte's *Madame Récamier de David*), with their Liquid Yeast Extract receptacles transforming into handles by which they will carry themselves to their ultimate destination. These bear no similarity to *love handles;* they are *death handles.*

Whom shall I call on? Who will share with me
The wretched happiness of staying alive?

—**Fyodor Dostoyevsky**, *Notes from Underground*

Graffito seen today at Voyagers: a phallus and a pair of lips, with the following inscription:

> To have a nice time first go to the Moon Under Water at
> Deansgate to have a few cheap drinks, then go to Fantasy
> Bar to see some lovely naked women for a tenner, and
> then go to a massage parlour to fuck a nice young whore.
> I did it and a young Paki whore with shaven cunt sucked
> me and I licked her as well.

Who said that "lavatorial graffiti are not to be distinguished
in any qualitative way from the drawings of Rembrandt or the
writings of Shakespeare"?

⁊⃗

> This idea of fun: cars, girls, Saturday night, bottle of
> wine... to me, those things are morbid.
>
> —**Morrissey** in John Robertson's *Morrissey In His Own Words*, p. 33

> Laughs without mirth.
> This is the death of the earth.
>
> —**T. S. Eliot**, *Little Gidding*, pt. 2, *in Four Quartets*

In the best of scenarios, the natives demonstrate symptoms of
acute gigglification (however, I hardly ever witnessed any instances
of *severe cachinnationism*) which is often the inevitable concomitant of brain-softening by means of various chemically challeng-
ing substances that may be drunk, smoked, inhaled, or, in exceptional circumstances, intravenously injected.

Indeed, the state of gigglification (or *having a laugh*) is much
sought after by the natives as it represents the hitherto scientifically acknowledged pinnacle of bliss. Well, given the quality
of fun in Brutland, should we blame Morrissey for the following statement?

> I would never, ever, do anything as vulgar as having fun.
>
> —**Morrissey**, *Morrissey In His Own Words*, by John Robertson, p. 25.

Perhaps the best description of what constitutes pleasure for the English can be found in Brian Harrison's book, *Drink and the Victorians*, (p. 338):

> Temperance reformers argued that the expansion in retail trades, from which many of them drew their livelihood, had superseded the commercial role of the fair; these occasions were now "not for the transacting of business of any kind, but merely for what is called *pleasure,* alias *drinking* ... gambling and fighting". [emphasis original]

And not to forget the brutological aspect of this survey:

> They well knew the violence and *brutality* which accompanied traditional recreations, some of which were deliberately promoted by self-interested publicans.
> [my emphasis]
>
> —*Ibid.,* p. 339

Within a century or so, food has changed, fashion has changed, destinations have changed. What about the attitude?

> The hype around Cool Britannia implies we've become a nation at ease with pleasure (in food, fashion and lifestyle, we've never had things so groovy). But there's another British face with which foreigners are all too familiar— the red one lying unconscious on the streets of Ibiza on the edge of a pool of vomit. This face of excess suggests we're more dumb brutes than cool Brits.
>
> —**Cosmo Landesman,** *"May we have the pleasure?",*
> *The Guardian,* 17/10/1998

Or perhaps tradition is stronger than ever:

> Yes kids, once again it's the annual carnage known as the UMIST Rag Beer Festival. Our... Bowling Green will be turned into the biggest drinking pit this side of Olly Reed's cellar on the 5th of November... in a re-enactment of the sort of behaviour that would put Eric the bloody Viking to shame.
>
> —*Grip,* p. 10

On the other hand, one can find such rare qualities as *compassion* and *pity* even in the heart of Brutland. Indeed, people who do not join in such metaphysical activities as boozing are considered cultural misfits and, as such, are eligible to receive the best help available for their unfortunate predicament:

> Historically speaking, Ye Olde UMISTe Beere Festivale was created so long ago that no one gives a flying f$@k how old it is, suffice it to say that if anyone tells you they've been to all of them, they are either a lying snot-gobbling dograt, or teetotal (in which case they may as well be put down out of pity).
>
> —*Grip*, p. 10

What do continentals believe about the way the Brits choose to amuse themselves?

> Referring to the alcoholic over-indulgences that sent Gazza to rehab clinic this week, Italy's leading sports paper, Gazetta dello Sport wrote: "In Italy, drunkenness has for centuries been the only socially reprehensible vice. It's not good to be seen staggering about in public. You lose face. But in England, for different cultural reasons, the habit of raising your right arm too often is not seen as something so unseemly, getting drunk is even seen as a synonym for entertainment; it is a basic component of Anglo-Saxon machismo". To many Europeans, the British are the barbaric Goths of mass tourism, interested only in going over the top.
>
> —**Cosmo Landesman**, "May we have the pleasure?",
> *The Guardian*, 17/10/1998

And why is it that the Brits should not worry about their habits and image?

> Those who worry should remember that drunkenness was once considered a normal part of our lives. Samuel Johnson said that when he was young "all the decent

people in Lichfield got drunk every night and were not the worse thought of". (...)

This over-exuberant relationship with alcohol remains a normal feature of British life—what's changed is society's attitude to it. The historian of English social life, Christopher Hibbert, says that in the 19th century "it was quite usual to see magistrates and members of parliament drunk on their benches".

—**Cosmo Landesman**, "May we have the pleasure?",
The Guardian, 17/10/1998

Well, talking about drunk MPs, is it just something that used to happen in those days of yore?

SIR NICHOLAS Scott, the former Tory minister, was found lying in a street in Bournemouth late on Wednesday night... "face down, kissing the pavement". Earlier in the evening, he had attended a reception, hosted by the Irish Embassy, where Guinness was free all night.

—*The Daily Telegraph,* 11/10/1995

The question, however, still remains, *why do the English choose to amuse themselves sadly?* The answered can be found in Engels, in his book, *The Condition of the Working Class in England* (1844):

They are goaded like wild beasts and never have a chance of enjoying a quiet life. They are deprived of all pleasures except sexual indulgence and intoxicating liquors. Every day they have to work until they are physically and mentally exhausted. This forces them to excessive indulgence in the only two pleasures remaining to them.

(*Quoted in Brian Harrison, Drink and the Victorians, p. 392*)

Well, if they had to choose between those two pleasures available to them, guess which one would be the winner:

I had locked my three children in the coal house and later
awoke in my neighbour's dog's kennel with a galvanised
bucket on my head. I have no money left and my wife has
left me. YOUR BEER FESTIVAL IS A WINNER!

—*Grip*, p. 11

Given that indulging in "intoxicating liquors" is perhaps the
main pleasure of the natives, and abstention might cause a nervous disorder with the concomitant effect of the loss of a good
labourer, native scientists have tried to substantiate scientifically
the fact that the "moderate" consumption thereof is not harm-
ful and even pregnant women can drink "a good pint" without
any remorse. Thus, on the first page of *The Times* of 3rd March
1997 we can read the headline: *Pregnant women may drink—in
moderation*; on the second page we see: *Pregnant women may
drink*; and on the ninth page we are reminded *once again* (!) with
another little article that *Drinking while pregnant is safe*. I don't
know about you, but I personally found this repetition—with its
rather strange variations—somewhat suspicious.

The business of America is business. The business of
Britain is very much living and enjoying life, the realisation
of a deeper and wider life outside the economic rat race.

—**Peter Grosvenor & James McMillan**, *The British Genius*, p. 534

Well, as a coda to the foregoing discussion I have to admit
that I must be seriously off my trolley, since in the land whose
business is very much living and enjoying life, I am still looking
for a native with whom I might be serious, after my fashion...
—or, even more to the point, with whom I might be *cheerful*!

A Gigantic Figure of an Aborted Embryo

The composite picture of man that emerges from the art of our time is the gigantic figure of an aborted embryo whose limbs suggest a vaguely anthropoid shape, who twists his upper extremity in a frantic quest for a light that cannot penetrate its empty sockets, who emits inarticulate sounds resembling snarls and moans, who crawls through a bloody muck, red froth dripping from his jaws, and struggles to throw the froth at his own non-existent face, who pauses periodically and, lifting the stumps of his arms, screams in abysmal terror at the universe at large.

—**Ayn Rand**, *The Romantic Manifesto*, p. 130

In the past, the English tried to impose a system wherever they went. They destroyed the nation's culture and one of the by-products of their systemization was that they destroyed their own folk culture.

—**Martin Carthy**, *The Guardian*, 29/12/1988

Some people, like me, don't want to be little Englanders. One of the things I most object to about the British music business is "Brit"—the stylization of culture in an intensely cynical way. The fact that most of the West speaks English has given us an inflated sense of our own self-importance... I live outside Dublin now, in the hills. It's the only place where I can play music really loud—otherwise I'd have to live in the suburbs. And you know what's wrong with that? They are full of English people.

—**Elvis Costello**, *GQ*, December 1996, p. 230

Fundamental idea of a commercial culture. Today one can see coming into existence the culture of a society of which *commerce* is as much the soul as personal contest was with the ancient Greeks and as war, victory and justice were for the Romans. The man engaged in commerce understands how to appraise everything without having made it, and to appraise it *according to the needs of the consumer*, not according to his own needs; "who and how many will consume this?" is his question of questions. This type of appraisal he then applies instinctively and all the time: he applies it to everything, and thus also to the productions of the arts and sciences, of thinkers, scholars, artists, statesmen, peoples and parties, of the entire age: in regard to everything that is made he inquires after supply and demand *in order to determine the value of a thing in his own eyes*. This becomes the character of an entire culture.

—**Friedrich Nietzsche**, *Daybreak*, p. 175

The things other people have put into *my* head, at any rate, do not fit together nicely, are often useless and ugly, are out of proportion with one another, are out of proportion with life as it really is outside my head.

I have no culture, no humane harmony in my brains. I can't live without a culture anymore.

—**Kurt Vonnegut**, *Breakfast of Champions*, p. 5

The English would be by far the first people on earth if they didn't lack two elementary and indispensable virtues for a civilized nation: a taste for good food and music.

—**Herman Hesse**, *Aforismi*, p. 82

Of the general inadequacy of intellect in the conduct of life Britain is the most majestic exponent. She is instinctively disliked by such people as French, Persians, Hindus, who are clever by nature, and think that *intellect can rule*. The Italians strayed down this path and disliked us too. But they, and the Greeks, and the Arabs, have a natural perception of other and greater powers and this, I think, is an affinity that binds us. With the others, with the intellectual, it is not our stupidity, but the fact that we prove it possible to live by non-intellectual standards, which makes us disliked.

—**Freya Stark**, *Perseus in the Wind*, ch. 4 (1948).

Of what use is a philosopher who doesn't hurt anybody's feelings?

—**Diogenes of Sinope**, *Herakleitos and Diogenes*, pt. 2, Fragment 10

hose who propound views that diverge from the norm are sworn at by means of the most abusive term existing in Brutish: *intellectual*. Intellectuals are not on a very good footing with the natives. Intellectuals, philosophers and poets are not exactly their *cup of tea*. Unless, of course, they occupy themselves with questions like whether or not the world has three dimensions, whether the mind has nine or twelve categories, or, simply, if they dedicate poems to the Queen.

Indeed, those who dedicate poems to the Queen get the best marks for their essays; they may even be given the title of *poet laureate*.

To quote from Dr Silentiarius' diary:

My initial belief had been that by joining Onanistan universities—be it the modest University of Central Petshire or the most prestigious universities of Cowbridge and Loxford—I would have the opportunity to rub shoulders with fellow Onanistan intellectuals. However, this proved to be as far from truth as Mars is from Earth. My mistake had been in assuming that the native universities would fulfil the same intellectual functions as the Martian universities. Not only were intellectuals hard to find, but even those who seemed to possess an iota of philosophic curiosity accepted unquestionably the native regime and culture. And what sort of intellectual conversation can you have in a filthy public house, standing amongst nauseous and nauseating semi-comatose inebriants with somebody who holds a pint of beer dearer than wholesome nutrition or the affections of a woman?

It is funny how "high art" manages to co-evolve with rather more popular aesthetics. The ghastliness of native attires is matched by a ghastliness in their art which, through a coetaneous evolution, achieves the much sought-after state of "contemporaneity" or *hipness*. Rumours have it that the Aesthetics of Ugliness (the "u" pronounced as "oo' in "moon" please) developed in one of Redbrick's Universities. Indeed, as I was tipped off by one of their Foul Art students, they are instructed by their professors to abandon the sentimentalism of portraiture and devote themselves to explorations of the abstract execrable.

The real weakness of England lies, not in incomplete armaments or unfortified coasts, not in the poverty that creeps through sunless lanes, or the drunkenness that brawls in loathsome courts, but simply in the fact that her ideals are emotional and not intellectual.

—**Oscar Wilde**, Gilbert, *in The Critic as Artist, pt. 2*

This is the country that invented two of the greatest gastro-
nomical concoctions of the century: *fisn 'n' chips* and *beans on
toast*; the country that celebrated courtly love by perfecting
the elusive art of *one-night stands*; the country that apotheo-
sized domesticated animals and remained gloriously apathetic
to human suffering; the country that replaced the joys and sorrows of social existence with the affective and intellectual poverty of the TV screen; the country that, in the wake of spirituality, found itself fast asleep... or gulping down pints.

   Culture, *anyone?*

They've Been Going In and Out of Style

To *dress down* is perhaps a peculiarly English verb, as only a native would feel the need to do so. "Glamour" here is a cause for suspicion—a low-key dress sense is needed in order to make you amiable and approachable amongst them. Lack of originality is always rewarded, perhaps as a form of art relevant to the general popularity enjoyed by the aesthetics of ugliness:

> Actively bad dressing may be an art raised to its highest form in England, but it is not within the reach of all as it requires a keen, if not misapplied, interest in fashion... The majority of Englishwomen regard the photographs in fashion magazines as having as much pertinence to them as the ones in *National Geographic* of Guatemalan tree frogs.
>
> —*Vogue*, January 1997, p. 88

Dressing down is also a moral imperative, as a dressed up person provokes the attention of the people on the basis of superficial qualities. And, of course, as a punishment for such an arrogant sartorial transgression, a dressed up person would be punished by being ostensibly unnoticed. In order to avoid such problems the locals often dress up by dressing down:

> They will continue to affect the costume of timeless dowdiness, usually involving a blazer and a floral skirt,

that may be seen in all occasions when Englishwomen
have consciously dressed up.

—*Vogue*, January 1997, p. 88

It is often remarkable to witness how English women dress up
when they go clubbing. It could be in the middle of the winter,
with a temperature below zero, and they will be dressed scant-
ily, without socks or stockings so that one can see their milky-
pink coloured feet.

I saw once a female student (was she a fine art student? I don't
know) who had been wearing trainers. So far, so good. But she
had chopped off their front, converting them into some sort
of postmodern flip-flops and fully exposing her naked toes. I
am sure that if I had taken more notes at the time I would have
come up with more detailed accounts of similar sartorial slips.
One thing is for sure however:

> Who can deny that to say that Englishwomen are badly
> dressed is putting it limply indeed? Not only are they a
> byword for that condition, but the phrase itself... falls
> short of the mark. It contains no hint of the intentional
> aesthetic assault in, for example, the persistent display of
> sheer navy-blue tights... They are probably illegal in Milan.
>
> —*Vogue*, January 1997, p. 88

Well, in Milan they may be illegal but the Italians don't really
need an aesthetic crime police. And the Brutish, who desper-
ately need one, simply don't have one! However, I have to confess: despite all that, or rather *because* of all that, the tights are
guaranteed to raise a smile—or a *grin*.

"I'm Gonna Kick Your Head In... — An "Innate Thuggishness"?

What people have to understand is that we're lads. We have burgled houses and nicked car stereos. We like girls and swear.
—**Noel Gallagher** of rock group Oasis, in *The Guardian*, 28/12/1996,
(The Year in Review by Catherine Bennett)

Wine-drinking countries have a steady pattern, while we get pissed out of our skulls on a Saturday night. In France they die of liver cirrhosis after a long period of pickling their livers—here problems tend to be seen in terms of violence and broken relationships
—*The Guardian*, 17/9/1996, "When life is just poured away"

And we are not the only people who indulge in racial stereotyping. To those excitable Latin types, to the suave French, and even to the punctilious Germans, the British are polite because they would be too embarrassed to be otherwise. The perceived other side of the British character is an innate thuggishness. (...)
Every year there is a depressingly familiar rash of attacks, thefts and other incidents marking the tensions between the foreign students and local youths. This year's ignominious highlight was the stabbing of a Russian student in a park west of Hove.

—*The Independent*, 30/8/1996

It also depresses me when people think they're part of some Great British heritage and they've got a God-given right to go ahead and beat people up if they can't get a pint and some chips at ten o'clock at night. It all came out again during Euro 96, didn't it? I mean, I was excited by England's performance and I really wanted them to win, but stabbing people after the match because they've got a German accent or they're driving an Audi—it's not really on, is it?

—**Jarvis Cocker**, *GQ*, December 1996, p. 187

English people are so peace-loving that they had devoted the last thousand years to knocking the hell out of people who *don't* like peace.

—**Peter Cagney**, *The Book of Wit and Humour*, 2596

I had been to a party. Fairly entertaining. People were dancing away carelessly, smoking their fags happily, drinking their beers and wines, chatting. Suddenly everything changed. A male of rather non-negligible proportions wanted to join in the party. However, the host had a different idea and as the fellow tried to push his way in, the host tried to push him out again. Temporarily our host seemed to be successful in that the intruder didn't insist on getting in.

After ten minutes, though, when he came back with a friend of his (also of non-negligible proportions) hell broke loose. They pushed their way in by punching the host in the face, proceeded into the main room, pulled out some rather ferocious-looking knives and started breaking anything that could be broken, stabbing the tables, the carpets, the wallpaper, shouting at the people "We're gonna foocking kill ye all!"

The girls were all gathered in a corner forming a little group, crying in each other's arms. Somebody said that he would call the police; this was not exactly poetry to their ears—its result was to fuel even more wrath and release more deeply repressed emotions. Practically, this meant that a few more people got punched in various parts of their bodies.

The whole thing lasted less than ten minutes. It swung from careless mirth to a condition of not knowing whether one would live for another five minutes. I thought to myself: This is Brutland—*by name and nature*!

⁂

Mrs Cheveley: ...a typical Englishman, always dull and usually violent.

—**Oscar Wilde**, *An Ideal Husband*

It was late on a Saturday night. My flatmate had returned from a night out clubbing—or, more correctly, from the casualties thereof. His hand was plastered. It transpired that he had had a fight in a club for no apparent reason. He confessed that he'd phoned up his girlfriend at three o'clock in the morning to boast that "it was fucking gorgeous". And everybody else in the flat thought of him as a hero.

Their frustration and repression is often released through such meretricious acts as the ritualistic breaking of bus-stop windows (an ad posted on a bus-stop window: "What if your granny was waiting to get the bus here?") and, especially, phone booths. And thank God this is an option. Luckily enough for many people, the breaking of phone booths and other inanimate structures was held up as the ultimate criterion of manhood, as a necessary inclusion in the repertoire of any alpha male, thus effectively sublimating the sexual drive and reducing the amount of harm to animate beings.

Another hobby which has to do with bus stops (non-violent this time) is *Bus Stop Climbing*. It is ever so popular with inebriated young natives, who will climb on top of bus stop roofs and make funny gestures and noises to vehicles and passers-by. This phenomenon reaches its peak during the *Gang Piss Up* (otherwise known as "New Year's Eve"). Native police, though, have ways of dealing even with this form of unacceptable and puerile behaviour. What do they do? They apply the so-called "anti-climb paint" on top and stick up a sign that reads (as seen in Dublin):

**Please do not climb. You will be prosecuted.
Anti-climb paint applied on top.**

꒰꒱

Before coming to Brutland I couldn't have imagined that the simple fact of being a university student could trigger phenomenal violence. The incident I am going to describe took place in the top deck of a bus that ran the "magic route" of student areas.

A few seats behind me there was a posse of three boys and two girls. The boys appeared sober (it was only nine o'clock) but they kept shouting abuse against students, along the lines of "students are dickheads" or "fuck students". It had been going on for about ten minutes when a student decided to get up and go downstairs in order to get off at the next stop. However, before walking down the stairs he glanced back at the abusive posse and made the all-too-eloquent sign, raising his middle finger while forming a fist with the rest of his hand. He didn't have to wait for long: the three males of the company charged him, punching and kicking him all the way down to the lower deck and out of the bus.

The bus driver resumed his trip as if nothing had happened.

Of course, I wouldn't have been that surprised by the above incident had I properly perused the alternative prospectus on Redbrick:

> Most city centre pubs are student-friendly, however "student-bashing" does exist as a phenomenon, and waffling on loudly about how you and Tarquin got sooooo pissed last night and couldn't be bothered going to any lectures, is as good as slapping a target on your face.
>
> —*The Sub Student Handbook,* p. 20

And funnily enough, the day after, I noticed a photocopy shop in Redbrick's Studentland which had a big sign reading: "STUDENT FRIENDLY" (see next page).

> English people are the most law-abiding in the world. Juvenile delinquency is practically unknown over the age of forty-two.
>
> —**Peter Cagney,** *The Book of Wit and Humour,* 2596

As part of my research I spent some time living in one of the more deprived areas of Redbrick. I will never forget the time

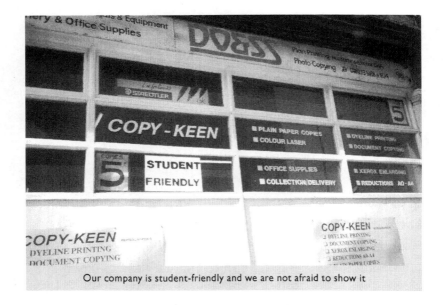

Our company is student-friendly and we are not afraid to show it

when I was attacked by a gang of ten- to twelve-year-olds ten metres away from the main entrance of my block. They were trying to trip me up for no apparent reason, maybe just for the fun and the devil of it. A few days later I received the local Newsletter which had the following article:

Mini Monsters!

Criminals come in all shapes, sizes, colours and sexes! You should be aware that gangs of kids are just as likely to commit a crime as teenagers and adults.

Not only do they bunch up and start vandalising things, but they are no less likely to commit acts of violence. A woman was recently attacked—kicked and punched— by a very young boy for no reason at all.

—The Courts Homewatch, [Hulme, Manchester], Issue 4, 12/1997

It is common knowledge that the main means of public transport in Brutland is the so-called *double-decker*. The double-decker is a type of bus with two levels, like the one involved in the aforementioned incident. The upper level can be accessed through a staircase. The official name of the upper level of a double-decker is *top-deck*. I have my own reasons to doubt the appropriateness of this term; in my opinion it is not true to its real purpose. Given that cannabis smokers all over the country (especially in the poorer areas) choose the upper level in order to exercise as discreetly as possible their right to inhale *shit*, I would recommend an inversion of the first component of the term "top-deck", in the form of an anagram, so that it may be truer to reality—that is to say *pot-deck*.

A paradigmatic example of the covert beastliness of the natives can be found in games specifically designed to harmlessly release pent-up emotions. Of course, such games are only allowed to sports people, with special emphasis on rugby players, who represent the *ne plus ultra* of native machismo. I will describe to you two of these games so that you can make up your own mind about them; their official names are *broomhandle* and *biscuit*.

For the game bearing the name of *broomhandle* we need two opponent teams of rugby players, a broom, and lots of pints (a *sine qua non,* I'm afraid). The teams are lined up a certain distance from the broom; a player from each team sets out to reach the broom, put its edge on his and his opponent's forehead, turn eight times around it, return, and drink a pint, with the same procedure followed by the next player of the team. The winning team is the one that drinks the pre-arranged number of pints first.

The second game is called *biscuit*. It is much simpler in the sense that less locomotion is involved and fewer parameters are employed. The team is sat around a biscuit. Each member begins to masturbate (*jack off, jerk off, toss, wank, wank off, beat off, whack off*), but frantically, because the one who ejaculates last will have to eat the biscuit.

                                   ❧

Indeed, if you still doubt the necessity of a specialized and fully accredited brutologist being involved in this research, if you do have any second thoughts about the old saying *homo est brutum bestiale*, then try catching a late night bus in Manchester on a Saturday night at the time when students return to Halls of Residence after clubbing.

                                   ❧

The following are some of the philosophical ruminations of Dr Silentiarius during his stay in Brutland:

> And if reliev'd, it is too often true,
> That they'll abuse their Benefactors too...
>
> —**Daniel Defoe**, *The True-Born Englishman*, Part 2, 552-3

> Be on your guard against the assaults your love makes upon you! The solitary extends his hand too quickly to anyone he meets.
>
> —**Friedrich Nietzsche**, "Of the Way of the Creator", *Zarathustra*

> I have to recogitate my old philosophy of never expecting anything good from Onanistan's humanoids even when you do something good for them (or should I say *especially* when you do something good for them). Not only should one not expect anything good from those humanoids; one should expect *the worst* imaginable. So one will be grateful if, without any motivation, they do something *simply bad* to one. In practical applications, one should be grateful to have been punched in the stomach and not in the face; or, one should be grateful to have been punched in the face but without breaking any glasses or teeth; or,

one should be grateful to have been punched in the face breaking glasses or teeth but without breaking the jaw (in any event, one should be grateful if only one rather than many teeth broke and, of course, if the glasses by breaking haven't seriously injured the eyes or caused blindness); or, one should be grateful to have been punched in the face and have one's jaw broken without having been stabbed in the stomach; or, one should be grateful to have been stabbed in the stomach and not in the chest or the reproductive organs; or, one should be grateful to have been stabbed in the chest or the reproductive organs but not in the heart; or, one should be grateful to have been stabbed only once in one place rather than many times in many places; or, one should be grateful that as the result of the stabbing one didn't bleed to death but had to spend three months in the hospital and six months at home recuperating afterwards—although perhaps one should be more grateful to *have been killed on the spot.*

To summarize:

I cannot but conclude the bulk of your natives to be the most pernicious race of little odious vermin that nature ever suffered to crawl upon the surface of the earth.

Jonathan Swift, *Gulliver's Travels*, Voyage to Brobdingnag, Chapter VI

Happy New Year... But Fuck Off Now Please!

11:00—the best closing time in the world?

—TV beer commercial

The TV used to shut down at midnight so we'd all be able to go to work the morning after—they didn't even trust us to go to bed on our own!

—**Shaun Ryder**, *GQ*, December 1996, p. 232

When I think of the hardship involved in only having seven hours to drink on a Sunday, my soul shudders.

—Government Minister **Kevin O'Higgins** speaking on the Intoxicating Liquor Bill, Ireland, 1927

Pubs and night-clubs will be able to stay open an extra hour on Fridays and Saturdays... the move is backed by the police and will almost complete the removal of pub licensing restrictions, introduced during the first world war to encourage sobriety among munition workers.

—*The Guardian*, 31/5/1996, "Extra hour for drinkers at weekends"

The English (it must be owned) are rather a foul-mouthed nation.

—**William Hazlitt**, *Table Talk*, "On Criticism" (1821–22).

*O*ne of the most traditional celebrations of the year in Brutland is considered to be *New Year's Eve* (otherwise known as *Gang Piss Up*). The first ten minutes of New Year's Day are probably the only 10 minutes during which the natives are likely to overcome—albeit temporarily—their reserve. If you are kissed by a woman it is a clear sign that she wants you to *get into her knickers*. The first hours of New Year's Day are when the highest number of accidents occur; when you see people climbing up bus stop roofs in order to perform their inebriated dance routines; when, for a lucky few, the dream of sex materializes in solid, *rat-arsed* reality.

It goes without saying that this major event is celebrated in pubs which, as a sign of generosity, extend their open hours past midnight. One New Year's, though, will never fade from my memory. At times it felt like a tragedy, and at times like a comedy. Sometimes something in between.

To cut a long story short, I had gone to a central pub of Redbrick with a couple of native friends of mine (some of my best friends are English). One of my friends, John, started chatting with an acquaintance of his, a girl who had come to the pub with her disabled aunt. Aunt was smoking a cigar in accordance with the local custom which allows such extravagant behaviour on a day like this.

Meanwhile her niece was flirting with a young man, and they started kissing. Aunt, still smoking her cigar, would interrupt every now and then, either because she wanted a light or because she just felt like having a chat with the young man. Niece was accommodating to aunt, despite the fact that aunt would interrupt at the most inopportune moments.

A few minutes later John went to the loo—only to return 15 minutes later with blood all over his forehead. "I started talking to this girl", he said, "and after a while a bloke came up to me and said, 'what the hell are you doing with my bird?' Without waiting for an answer, he raised his bottle of beer, which soon afterwards landed on my head. He went absolutely mental."

My other friend, Brian, went to the hospital with John who apparently needed a few stitches. It was five to twelve. The show had to go on. At twelve o'clock the natives started kissing each other (!) and sang the traditional tune:

> Should auld acquaintance be forgot
> And never brought to mind?
> Should auld acquaintance be forgot,
> And auld lang syne!
> For auld lang syne, my jo,
> For auld lang syne,
> We'll take a cup of kindness yet
>
> For auld lang syne...

After that, time went by pretty fast. It was about one o'clock. Everybody was sufficiently pissed by now to ignore the publican's cries:

We've had your money now everybody
FUCK OFF NOW PLEASE!

People ignored him. His language didn't seem to bother them. Would it have bothered them if they were not drunk? Somebody tried to get another drink from the bar. He got a dodgy look. "We don't serve anymore".

The publican started cleaning the pub despite the fact that most people were still inside. He repeated:

I know "Happy New Year" and all that but
GO OUTSIDE NOW PLEASE!

The natives reluctantly abandoned their half-finished pints (some took them out with them) and left in a drunken and disorderly manner.

Now, this made the publican happy.

We're Sergeant Peppers Lonely Hearts Club Band...

The English are so nice
so awfully nice
they are the nicest people in the world.

And what's more, they're very nice about being nice
About your being nice as well!
If you're not nice they soon make you feel it.

Americans and French and Germans and so on
They're all very well
But they're not *really* nice, you know.
They're not nice in *our* sense of the word, are they now?

That's why one doesn't have to take them seriously
We must be nice to them of course,
Of course, naturally.
But it doesn't really matter what you say to them,
They don't really understand.
You can just say anything to them:
Be nice you know, just nice
But you must never take them seriously, they wouldn't
understand,
Just be nice, you know! Oh, fairly nice,
Not too nice of course, they take advantage
But nice enough, just nice enough
To let them feel they're not quite as nice
as they might be.

—**D. H. Lawrence**, The English are so nice!

The Germans are called brutal, the Spanish cruel, the Americans superficial, and so on; but we are perfide Albion, the island of hypocrites, the people who have built up an Empire with a Bible in one hand, a pistol in the other, and financial concessions in both pockets. Is the charge true? I think it is.

—**E. M. Forster**, *Notes on the English Character*

*T*he national collective unconscious suffers greatly from the symptoms of a disease called "Acute Colony Deprival Syndrome". In stricter psychological terms I would define this affliction as "the remnants of a previous superiority complex which has been compounded in order to hide the current inferiority complex". Although methadone has been administered, in the form of *Falkland Islands* and *Hong Kong*, the imminent withdrawal of the latter has had no therapeutic effect whatsoever. The craving for heroin is still the same—exacerbated by the withdrawal of methadone—sorry, I actually meant "the withdrawal of *Hong Kong*". An eternity without colonies then, from now on— and should they have the right to...

s m i l e ?

৯

Give a monkey a brain and he'll think he is the centre of the universe.

—*Martian Holy Scripture*

In Brutland there is a widespread belief that the other countries of the world—commonly referred to as *overseas*—revolve around it like ornamental satellites in an orderly and insignificant manner. Such a Brutocentric view of the world has never been challenged within its territory, for excommunication would certainly be the punishment. And, of course, wherever they go, the natives have to affirm their alleged superiority:

> The English in Greece—a sorry lot, by the way—seem to have a poor opinion of the Greek character. The English are torpid, unimaginative, lacking in resiliency. They seem to think that the Greeks should be eternally grateful to them because they have a powerful fleet. The Englishman in Greece is a farce and an eye-sore: he isn't worth the dirt between a poor Greek's toes.
>
> —**Henry Miller**, *The Colossus of Maroussi*, p. 39

> To identify with "British" is not the same as identifying with the warmth and width of English, Scottish, Welsh or Irish. "British" is a limited, utilitarian allegiance simply to those political and legal institutions which still hold this multi-national state together.
>
> —**Bernard Crick**, *The Independent*, 22/5/1993

> Englishness, a rich compound, now emerged in the more conventional form of English nationalism. It had a narrowness and, occasionally, a fanaticism generally absent from the older Englishness. It opposed itself now not just to the continental Europeans and to the Irish and Scots but more explosively to the people of non-English origin in its midst. Essentially it is a version of "Little Englandism", almost, one might say, of tribalism.
>
> —**Krishnan Kumar**, *"Britishness" and "Englishness":*
> *What prospect for a European identity in Britain today?*, from British Studies,
> (ed) Nick Wadham Smith, the British Council, 1995, p. 93

The British as a nation actually do not exist (especially since the collapse of the British Empire). Ask a Scot (otherwise known as *Jocks*): will he call himself a *Briton*? And what about the Welsh (otherwise known as *Taffs*), or the Irish (otherwise known as *Paddies*)? And finally, what about the most dominant and arrogant of the subspecies, the English (otherwise known as *Sassenachs* or more colloquially as *Bastards*), would they call themselves British? Indeed as Mr Fowler says:

> It must be remembered that no Englishman... calls himself a Briton without a sneaking sense of the ludicrous, or hears himself referred to as a Britisher without squirming. How should an Englishman utter the words *Great Britain* with the glow of emotion that for him goes with England? His sovereign may be Her *Britannic* Majesty to outsiders, but to him is Queen of *England*; he talks the *English* language; he has been taught *English* history as one continuous tale from Alfred to his own day; he has heard of the word of an *Englishman* and aspires to be an *English* gentleman; and he knows that *England* expects every man to do his duty... In the word *England*, not in *Britain* all these things are implicit. It is unreasonable to ask forty millions of the people to refrain from the use of the only names that are in tune with patriotic emotion...
>
> —**H.W. Fowler**, *A Dictionary of Modern English Usage*,
> 2nd edition revised by Sir Ernest Gowers (1965)

Apart from royalty, only military officers, politicians, journalists, demented Old Age Pensioners and the like utilize the highly artificial terms *British* or *Briton*. And perhaps the mere existence of royalty is the major booster (with the assistance of both "lowbrow" and "highbrow" media) of the fictitious nature of the British National Identity. Perhaps a more apt term for the infamous United Kingdom is *Divided Kingdom*. (more in: John Osmond's *The Divided Kingdom*; see also H. Kearney: *The British Isles: a history of four nations*).

And if United Kingdom is an infamous term then what about "Great Britain"? Without the empire it sounds rather insubstantial and anachronistic. And it is amazing how Great Britain shrunk into "Little England"; or is it that, deep down, on a psychological plane of existence, it has always been so? What about its pomposity, its royal simulacra, being nothing more but a cover of this little-England-mindedness?

Much of the language of Britishness, and many of the attitudes, in the recent period, have to do with the British Empire and the sense of Britain's imperial role in the world [...] The old British passport, with its lofty language about "Her Britannic Majesty" requesting this and that, well epitomizes this imperial aspect of Britishness.

—**Krishnan Kumar,** "Britishness and Englishness:
What prospect for a European identity in Britain today?", from
British Studies, (ed) Nick Wadham Smith, the British Council, 1995, p. 87

Last but not least, a very interesting way of explaining the decline of British Empire (and the decline of its social *mores*) can be found in the chapter "Buggery and the Decline of the British Empire" in Christie Davies' book *Permissive Britain.*

With regard to the social *mores,* we can say that ex-colonies, at least, can be useful once again, serving now as examples:

Once we sailed forth to civilize the natives; now we look to Southeast Asia for models of social discipline.

—**Lesley White,** "Riot Acts", *The Sunday Times Magazine,* 21/7/1996, p. 46

"English Malady" or "Cognitive Dissonance"?

The title I have chosen for this Treatise, is a Reproach universally thrown on this Island by Foreigners, and all our Neighbours on the Continent, by whom nervous Distempers, Spleen, Vapours, and Lowness of Spirits, are in Derision, called the ENGLISH MALADY. And I wish there were not so good Grounds for this Reflection. The Moisture of our Air, the Variableness of our Weather, (from our Situation amidst the Ocean) the Rankness and Fertility of our Soil, the Richness and Heaviness of our Food, the Wealth and abundance of the Inhabitants (from their universal Trade) the Inactivity and sedentary Occupations of the better Sort (among whom this Evil mostly rages) and the humour of living in great, populous and consequently unhealthy Towns, have brought forth a Class and Set of distempers, with atrocious and frightful Symptoms, scarce known to our Ancestors, and never rising to such fatal Heights, nor afflicting such Numbers in any other known Nation. These nervous disorders being computed to make almost one third of the Complains of the People of Condition in England...

—**George Cheyne**, *The English Malady; or, A Treatise of Nervous Diseases of all Kinds, with the Author's Own Case* (1733)

Britain! Infamous for suicide!
An island in thy manners! Far disjoin'd
From the whole world of rationals beside!

—**Edward Young**, *Night Thoughts*, Night v, 1. 442

Plainly many late seventeenth-century Englishmen shared an obsessive yet apprehensive view of sexuality. For all their libertine philosophising and summonses to merriment, they seem profoundly inhibited and uncomfortable about the subject. They cannot treat it in a matter-of-fact, balanced, way; they cannot laugh about it without sniggering, or describe it straightforwardly, joyously, even innocently. Their reaction is disproportionate, discordant, distorted and disassociated.

—**Roger Thompson**, *Unfit for Modest Ears*, p. 210,
as quoted by **Paul-Gabriel Boucé** (ed) in *Sexuality in eighteenth-century Britain*,
Manchester UP, 1982, p. 3

An American journalist with the magazine Vanity Fair recently said to me: "I can't figure the British out—they're either getting smashed out of their skulls or sitting around sipping tea. There doesn't seem to be anything in the middle of these two extremes".

—**Cosmo Landesman**, "May we have the pleasure?",
The Guardian, 17/10/1998

England is nothing but the last ward of the European madhouse, and quite possibly it will prove to be the ward for particularly violent cases.

—**Leon Trotsky**, *Diary in Exile* (1959), entry for 11/4/1935.

For Allah created the English mad—the maddest of all mankind!

—**Rudyard Kipling**, *Kitchener's School*

We do not regard Englishmen as foreigners. We look on them only as rather mad Norwegians.

—**Halvard Lange**, *The Observer*, 9/3/1957

Rather than hypocrisy, it is a form of *cognitive dissonance*—
that is to say that the British hold two incompatible beliefs
with equal conviction. On the one hand, we seem to have
an easy-going acceptance of the fun of sex. We also seem
to allow for differences in people's sexuality... on the other,
we seem to be repelled by it: Sex is the sinful, squelching,
"bonking" two-backed beast. [My emphasis]

—*The Observer*, 13/10/1996

What intellectual arguments can one put against my consider-
ing the expression *cognitive dissonance* a refined euphemism for
the more straightforward term, *schizophrenia?* For, despite its
nosological connotations, etymologically speaking, it denotes
nothing more than a split mind, an inability to navigate the
dichotomy between fantasy and reality:

From the clinical point of view, schizophrenia takes a
variety of apparently very disparate forms. The following characteristics are the ones usually picked out as typical: *incoherence of thought, action and affectivity; detachment from reality* accompanied by *a turning in upon the self*
and the predominance of *a mental life given over to the
production of fantasies;* a delusional activity which may be
marked in a greater or lesser degree, and which is always
badly systematised. Lastly, any disease which evolves at
the most variable of paces towards an *intellectual and
affective "deterioration".* [My emphasis]

—**Laplanche, J. & Pontalis, B.,** *The Language of Psychoanalysis,*
Karnac and the Institute of Psychoanalysis,
1988, see entry for "schizophrenia".

Now, I shall attempt an analysis of all these traits with respect
to key attitudes, expressions, quotations, and clichés that can be
found in, for, and about, the native culture:

1) *incoherence of thought, action and affectivity*—"and, what is worse, the same disorder in ideas, in talk, in feeling"

—George Bernard Shaw, *Heartbreak House*, Act I, Lady Utterword

2) *detachment from reality*—"But they're [the English] sort of dislocated from reality—and terribly repressed about everything".

—Bryan Magee, *Facing Death*, p. 77

3) *a turning in upon the self*—"every man is an island" (a distortion of Donne's "no man is an island"); "keep yourself to yourself"; "keep one's distance".

4) *a mental life given over to the production of fantasies*— "It's as if the whole country's missing out on life".

—Bryan Magee, *Facing Death*, p. 77

5) *intellectual and affective "deterioration"*—"don't like showing my emotions'; "stiff upper lip"; "give somebody the cold shoulder".

Naturally, *cognitive dissonance* is not necessarily the only nor the best euphemism which describes the English malady. Forster defined English hypocrisy as *unconscious deceit* and *muddle-head-edness*. Another one, and a better one, is a bit of a mouthful but worth mentioning here:

> The British character is an amalgam of Puritan thrift, sobriety, self-help with not a little humbug, and a joyous abandon of restraints when the puritanism becomes too irksome. Not by accident did England pioneer the mini-skirt while retaining stern licensing laws for the sale and consumption of liquor.
>
> —**Peter Grosvenor & James McMillan**, *The British Genius*, p. 15

Of course, it is not at all easy to define this certain *je ne sais quoi* of the British psyche. Only through recourse to contradictory statements can we get closer to the truth:

> Sometimes it's hard to tell if we are now a nation of happy hedonists—or puritanical hypocrites.
>
> —**Cosmo Landesman**, "May we have the pleasure?",
> *The Guardian*, 17/10/1998

It is quite interesting that although they are liberal enough to have the so-called "gay/lesbian and bisexual" societies at Universities (something which would cause a scandal in most continental countries), they seem to be incapable of making a pass at each other (equally valid for homosexuals as well as heterosexuals) unless they are totally off their heads. And when they do it, it usually ends in a one-night-stand or a disastrous relationship.

What can be done, then, to remedy this rather unhealthy state of mind, this "cognitive dissonance"? One way of remedying it is the so-called serotonin re-uptake inhibitors—a trendy type of antidepressants. Indeed, this family of anti-depressants has been found to give women spontaneous orgasms upon sneezing, thus relieving cognitively dissonant women from the necessity of achieving cognitive consonance before they can climax. Indeed, this is a good way of explaining why the natives are so attached to both their depressive and their sneezing habits.

It would be quite a surprise if the language of the natives did not reflect in its diversity that "cognitively dissonant" state of mind which is so characteristic of them. The following list is by no means all-conclusive:

a bit touched, all over the board, a roo loose in the top paddock, around the bend, a sandwich short of a picnic, a square peg in a round hole, a tinny short of an eight pack, balmy, bananas, barmy, batty, bats, batshit, bats in the belfry, boho, boners, bourbon, bughouse, cracked, crackers, cracko, crazy, crazy-arse, cruising with one's lights on dim, cuckoo, daffy, dingnoat, dippy, doofus, doolally, dopey, dorky, dotty, freaky, gaga, gone, half-cracked, half gone, half-there, harpic, has a few of his pages stuck together, has a tile loose, kooky, lakes, lamebrained, loco, loony, loopy, loose up top, mad, mad as a hatter, mad as a March hare, mental, neuro, non compos, not all there, not quite there, not right in the head, (not having) both oars in the water, not playing with a full deck, nutter, nut case, nuts, nutso, nutty (as a fruitcake), off-beat, off-brand, off one's base, off one's bean, off one's block, off one's cake, off one's chump, off one's dip, off one's dot, off one's head, kadoova, off one's kazip, off one's nana, off one's nob, off one's nut, off one's onion, off one's pannican, off one's rocker, off one's rocket, off one's saucer, off one's top, off one's top traverse, off one's trolley, off the beam, off the wall, out in left field, out of one's box, out of one's cake, out of one's chump, out of one's head, out of one's gourd, out of one's kelter, out of one's nut, out of one's onion, out of one's rocker, out of one's mind, out of one's onion, out of one's tree, out of whack, out to lunch, plumb loco, potty, only eighty pence in the pound, queer as a coot, queer as a nine-bob note, Radio Rental, round the bend, round the twist, rum, schitzi, screwy, sicko, squirrelly, stark staring bonkers, touched, touched in the head, two bricks short of the load, two pence short of a bob, twisted, unglued, unhinged, unbalanced, wacko, wacky, whack-a-doo, whacked out, whacko, whacky, weird, wig city, wigged out, wiggy, wild, wild-arse, wingding, (living in a) worm farm, wired, yampi, zany...

Happiness is a Cigar Named Hamlet

If we possess our why of life we can put up with almost any *how*.—Man does not strive after happiness; only the Englishman does that.

—**Friedrich Nietzsche**, *Twilight of the Idols*, I 12

The British do not expect happiness. I had the impression, all the time that I lived there, that they do not want to be happy; they want to be right.

—**Quentin Crisp**, *Love Lies Bleeding*
(published in *New Statesman and Society*, 9/8/1991; first broadcast 6/8/1991)

How hard it is to make an Englishman acknowledge that he is happy!

—**Thackeray**, *Perdennis*, Book ii, chapter 31

An unknown woman telephoned me from England to complain that she was unhappy. To be a woman, to be unknown and to live in England is a triple burden of grief almost too heavy to support.

—**Quentin Crisp**,"The only emotion to be sure of is fear",
The Guardian, 6/12/1996

Happiness is predicated upon consumption, and the only virtuous activity is material enrichment.

—*The Guardian*, 27/12/1994,
"Happiness that money truly cannot buy"

Life is essentially a cheat and its conditions are those of defeat... the redeeming things are not "happiness and pleasure" but the deeper satisfactions that come out of struggle.

—**F. Scott Fitzgerald** (said shortly before his death)

If we try to adjust ourselves intentionally in some way, it is impossible to be natural. If you try to adjust yourself in a certain way, you will lose yourself. So without any intentional, fancy way of adjusting yourself, to express yourself freely as you are is the most important thing to make yourself happy, and to make others happy.

—**Shunryun Suzuki**, *Zen Mind, Beginner's Mind*, p. 89

 concept similar to the French *joie de vivre* (or even *bon viveur*); the Italian *allegria* (or *dolce vita*—which funnily enough has pejorative connotations in English); or the Greek εὖ ζῆν (the good life) is indeed conspicuous by its absence—not only in the English dictionary of words but *especially* in the English dictionary of *emotions*. And it makes sense: i.e. if one hasn't got the signified to start with what's the need for the signifier?

But perhaps the gravest gap of them all (should I call it a "cultural" gap?) is the lack of a word to indicate erotic love, a word like *amore*, *amour*, or *eros*. Again, it makes absolute sense: if there is no actual emotion that can be identified with the concept, then why should the concept exist?

※

Perhaps one of the greatest psychological barriers to their enjoyment of life is the natives' all-encompassing guilt complex. It is as if guilt is an inevitable corollary of pleasure. And it is this conditioned reflex, this *Victorian Pavlov's dog*, that led to the creation of ARISE (Associates for Research into the Science of Enjoyment). This is an international association whose founder is—of course—English, and whose aim is to research the idea of pleasure. According to their findings, the most guilt-ridden people are the Australians, closely followed by the Germans and the British (*Lakeside* magazine, February 1997, Vol. 4, issue no 2).

※

Sometimes the media try to awaken the natives from their depressive lethargy, especially when they advertise holiday destinations like "España, a Passion for Life". One can easily infer that you can flee to a place where there is passion for life only from a place where there is none.

> The students of English too must be of university qual-
> ity, capable of a high level of work and with a genuine and
> intelligent interest in literature, and secondly, the perma-
> nent school must be staffed with seniors *qualified to take*
> *pleasure in "teaching"* such pupils—that is, to find working
> with them a profitable kind of collaboration.

[My emphasis]

—**F.R. Leavis**, *English Literature in our time and the University*, p. 3-4

Enough of Academic qualifications. What the people of this country really need is vocational qualifications. A BNVQ in happiness training should be introduced as a first step. Then, the old, academic courses, such as BAs and BScs, should be replaced by the unified approach of BH (Bachelor of Happiness). Thus, one would not get a BA in English Literature, but a BH in English Literature, that is to say, the aforementioned subject would be studied if, above anything else, it would greatly increase the students' happiness. Consequently, the students would not need GCEs or anything of the sort as entrance qualifications; they would simply need passion for their chosen subject, a critical mind, and a lot of reading behind them. Naturally, this implies that the teachers would practive their profession for the sheer bliss they experienced in doing so. Teachers that were not delir-ious about teaching and students not delirious about learning would not have a place in the new system.

To those for whom the only instigation to thought is a balance sheet, I will try to make the above argument relating to happiness training more acceptable by presenting it under the guise of a business proposition: O*ne should not forget that happiness train-ing can be pretty big business indeed.*

Of course, there are many happy English people. You'll find

them in all walks of life (that lead to a nursery) all ages (under four) and all over the world (apart from England). Exaggerating?

> Personality, particularly a sanguine temperament, is a powerful influence on happiness but here we find that British phlegmaticism has been undermined by the neurosis-inducing activities of the health fanatics who have managed to persuade so many of us that the innocent pleasures of food, alcohol and sex are harmful, if not downright dangerous. (...)

> Dr Bentall points out, happiness is caused by disturbances of the central nervous system and can be induced by epileptic seizures or by stimulating a discreet area of the left hemisphere of the brain. (...) "Happiness meets all reasonable criteria for a psychiatric disorder. It is statistically abnormal, it reflects abnormal functioning and is associated with a lack of contact with reality".

> —*The Times*, June 8, 1993, "Will sunshine cheer us up?"

No wonder then that:

> In Britain one in fifty doctors are said to commit suicide...

> —**Jan de Vries**, *Stress and Nervous Disorders*, p. 68

I have concluded that the natives demonstrate the same allergic reaction to happiness as they exhibit to the rare sightings (even rarer if it rains on St Swithin's day) of unobfuscated solar radiation. Symptoms range from a redness of the skin, followed by the inevitable peeling, headaches and hangovers (the latter exacerbated by the combined forces of sun and beer), to "healthy looking" melanoma. From this we might be led to conclude that *happiness is a warm sun*; however, being cognisant of the early evening hours in Brutland, the so called "happy hours" during which booze is discounted, I would more readily assert that *happiness is a warm pint*.

A conclusion reinforced by the fact that a dictionary definition of the word "happy" is "slightly intoxicated". (*Collins English Dictionary*, Millenium Edition, p. 703).

Affection as a Synonym for Affectation

One should never direct people towards happiness, because happiness too is an idol of the market-place. One should direct them towards mutual affection. A beast gnawing at its prey can be happy too, but only human beings can feel affection for each other, and this is the highest achievement they can aspire to.

—**Alexander Solzhenitsyn:** Shulubin in *Cancer Ward*, pt. 2, ch. 10

The teaching of Personal and Social Education (PSE) in schools has never been more necessary, but can we really show a nation of mistrustful individuals how better to relate with others, when others, especially the young, are clearly seen as the enemy?

—**Lesley White,** "Riot Acts", *The Sunday Times Magazine*, 21/7/1996, p. 44-5

The loss of spontaneous expression in children, the first and most important manifestation of the final sexual suppression, takes place in the fourth to fifth year of life. This quality is always first experienced as "dying", "being armoured", or "being immured", or "being dead" may be later partially compensated for by camouflaging psychic attitudes, e.g., *superficial joviality* or *contactless sociability*. [My emphasis]

—**Wilhelm Reich**, *The Function of the Orgasm*, p. 302

Preston: What's the point of your existence?
Mary: To feel. Cause you've never done it, you can never know it. But it's as vital as breath. And without it—without love, without anger, without sorrow—breath is just a clock ticking.

—**Equilibrium** (The Movie)

I am not glad. The natural term of the affection of the human animal for its offspring is six years. My daughter Ariadne was born when I was forty-six. I am now eighty-eight. If she comes, I am not at home. If she wants anything, let her take it. If she asks for me, let her be informed that I am extremely old and have totally forgotten her.

—**G. B. Shaw**, *Heartbreak House*, Act I (spoken by The Captain)

Openly indulging in affection for somebody is a cause of extreme embarrassment in Brutland. The natives are quick to discharge any duties of "affection" (affectation) that are institutionally (formally) owed to others—their children, for example. Even this relationship of *consanguinity* fails to break the mould of formalized behaviour with its irrevocable distancing, detachment, and *de-familiarization*, which occur when the child has come of age (or even sooner).

I was in the bus when I saw a young lady wearing a rather interesting badge pinned on her jacket. It read: *Hug Therapist*. It was as if I had seen a ray of light in the pitch darkness of Acheron. I thought to myself, "This country needs quite a few million of these in order to achieve some basic state of humanization". Indeed, I couldn't imagine anybody on Mars wearing a badge like that; it would be like trying to promote water as a liquid that is necessary for survival.

I feel as though there's no love here somehow [hand over heart]. And my husband or my mother, although we got on very well, and I thought a lot of her but I just feel as though I've no love. And, er, it's a horrible fear. I feel terribly guilty about it... terribly guilty about it. It's just as

> though here it's just empty. Absolutely empty. And I keep
> thinking... well there must be something wrong with me
> [...] I want to show them love and yet I don't feel love
> here, and I know I should do. It doesn't seem natural. It's
> not natural is it?
>
> —Freda in **Robert Hobson's** *Forms of Feeling*, p. 27

So, what is meant by "sex"? Oh, sex is not just "sex", it is the grand metaphor—for *affection*; affection and the uninhibited manifestation thereof in *every* conceivable way.

Without sex (in a relationship without emotional bonding) one can *survive* for 100 years; without affection (emotional bonding) one cannot *truly* live for a single moment.

Affectionlessness is the condition of one who, usually without realising it, has *dropped out of life*. And this sort of death-in-life is a million times more tragic than actual death.

Beautiful Boy...

FOUR out of ten children will suffer from mental illness... The figure includes problems ranging from eating disorders to suicide attempts.

—*The Times*, 2/12/1996

An English childhood is something to be got over as quickly as possible. To be an English grown-up—that is the only really glorious thing.

—**Antony Miall**, *Xenophobe's Guide to the English*, p. 22

We are a lukewarm people for all our feast days and hard work. Not much touches us, but we long to be touched. We lie awake at night willing the darkness to part and show us a vision. Our children frighten us in their intimacy, but we make sure they grow up as us.

—**Jeanette Winterson**, *The Passion*, p. 7

How many times have I wondered if it is possible to forge links with a mass of people when one has never had strong feelings for anyone, not even one's own parents; if it is possible to have a collectivity when one has not been deeply loved oneself by individual human creatures. Hasn't this had some effect on my life as a militant—has it not tended to make me sterile and reduced my quality as a revolutionary by making everything a matter of pure intellect, of pure mathematical calculation?

—**Antonio Gramsci**

Only an Englishwoman would want her daughter to be more comfortable with a horse than a man. And sadly it works. Sexual segregation is the source of all our gaucheness. By the time we are 16 it's too late: the atmosphere of sexual appraisal is alien to us...

—*Vogue*, January 1997, p. 89

*T*he young of the species undergo a rigid training regime from a very tender age in order to attain control of their unsavory affective manifestations. They are guided in the mystic art of building up and developing a potent neuromuscular armor that will safely lock—or even extinguish—all unwelcome manifestations of emotion. As a result of that, a number of catch-phrases have come about denoting aboriginal status, like: "stiff upper lip", "give somebody the cold shoulder", etc. Hence, the typical countenance of a native is that of *rigidly adhered-to unexpressiveness.*

Children are the same anywhere in the world. You see, they are pre-cultural beings, they *predate* culture, they *defy* culture, and at the same time they have a precious little culture of their own: one of spontaneous energy, unhindered emotion and unfabricated bliss. It is such a pity that English children, when they grow up, will have to become English adults! Otherwise, in order to escape adult senility, a philosophically inclined individual would, I suppose, have to opt for a conscious regression into infancy.

Jonathan Swift in his "Modest Proposal" recommended that the young ones of Ireland should be used to feed the starving population. Of course, his writing was a satirical attempt to increase people's awareness regarding the conditions in Ireland. Two and a half centuries later similar proposals are being put forth, but this time for real:

If intolerance really has to be the spirit of this age, *The Economist* would like to suggest restrictions on another source of noise pollution: children. (...) Anybody who has suffered a 12-hour flight with a bawling baby in the row immediately ahead or a bored youngster viciously kicking their seat from behind, will grasp this as quickly as they would love to grasp the youngster's neck. Here is a clear case of market failure: parents do not bear the full costs (indeed young babies travel free), so they are too ready to take their noisy brats with them. Where is the invisible hand when it is needed to administer a good smack?

The solution to this problem is obvious according to the writer's market-oriented logic:

All airlines, trains and restaurants should create child-free zones... instead of letting children pay less and babies go free, they should be charged (or taxed) more than adults, with the revenues used to subsidise seats immediately in front of the war-zone.

Passengers could then request a no-children seat, just as they now ask for a no-smoking one. As more women choose not to have children and the number of older people without young children increases, the demand for child-free travel will expand. Well, yes, it is a bit intolerant—but why shouldn't parents be treated as badly as smokers?

—*The Economist*, 5/12/1998:
"Mum's the word: When children should be screened and not heard"

Well, it is not very surprising that when the reproduction rates of the country are going down, children, like passion, are not exactly in vogue.

Touch Me Not!

It is not that the Englishman can't feel—it is that he is afraid to feel. He has been taught at his public school that feeling is bad form. He must not express great joy or sorrow, or even open his mouth too wide when he talks—his pipe might fall out if he did.

—**E. M. Forster**, *Abinger Harvest*, "Notes on the English character"

I had a wonderful two weeks in Turkey. The landscape and specially the warmth of the people really seduced me. Oh, if only the English could know how much more delightful and nourishing human contact can be with just a bit more of closeness and physical contact... It was brilliant to be in a country where men touch and kiss each other naturally as part of greeting and parting. The only previous experience of it had been my two-month stay in Marseilles a few years ago. Does that happen in Greece too?

—An e-mail from **F. G.**, a Brazilian friend

Why people don't touch? People should touch more...

—Uttered by a non-tactile native during a tactile awareness millisecond

In Brutland *touch* shifts between two levels of signification: it can be interpreted either as *sex* or *violence*. Touch, perceived as an act of natural *affection*, in an ordinary, day-to-day context, (especially at a same-sex, man-to-man level) is *well out of order*: it would be like forcing a superimposed level of transcendental signification down the sore throat of a secularised society. However, sometimes both these levels can coexist, so that we have both sex and violence, as is the case with Emma, Jane Austen's heroine:

> Scarcely had they passed the sweep-gate and joined the other carriage, than she found her subject cut up—her hand seized—her attention demanded, and Mr. Elton actually making violent love to her...
>
> —**Jane Austen**, *Emma*, chapter XV

Only that "make violent love" here simply means to engage in passionate courtship—in short, just an example of overinflated language:

> ...availing himself of the precious opportunity, declaring sentiments which must be already well known, hoping— fearing—adoring—ready to die if she refused him...

> And that is... how they are. So terribly physically all over one another. They pour themselves one over the other like so much melted butter over parsnips. They catch each other under the chin, with a tender caress of the hand, and they smile with sunny melting tenderness into each other's face.
>
> —**D. H. Lawrence** *Sea and Sardinia*, ch. I (1923), of the Sicilians.

It is so easy to make a cultural *faux pas* when you've been away from a life-castrating country for some time. I had been in southern France to see some friends and as you probably know people there have the habit of kissing each other socially, as a greeting—*la bise*, as the custom is called. I should note that you are allowed to kiss even with people whom you meet for the first time. The only difference is the number of times you are meant to kiss, as it varies, according to the region, from 2 to 4. Now, the worst *faux pas* you can make in France is trying to kiss three times in a region where two is the standard. Naturally, nobody will get the wrong idea or feel insulted if something like this happens.

On the other hand, the *faux pas* in England is *daring to kiss at all*. Having gained the kissing momentum in France I was unmindful enough to perform a similar practice with a girl I knew in England—we were staying in the same Halls of Residence. You can imagine what ensued: she was utterly shocked. The day after, she invited me for a talk about the incident claiming that my behaviour was not correct and that I should apologise!

༚

Men, on the other hand, are not much better when it comes to flirtation or warmth. Once I expressed my admiration for a woman to a male friend of mine by saying, "Look, a beautiful woman!"

What did he do? He didn't even turn his head round, he only murmured "one-track mind, mate..."

༚

After painstaking observation I concluded that the most tactile groups belonged to the underworld—such as punks, for example. "That must be why natives think them so low" I thought. Although I did admire the liberal and spontaneous non-sexual tactility of such groups, I wondered about the impossible logistics of erotic tactility—especially if they both share a number of rings in their lips, noses, tongues, and other perhaps more intimate parts of their bodies.

Some religious groups with Eastern origins also demonstrated a higher than usual degree of tactility. Indeed, I find that the two very different groups (punks and mystics) have a great deal in common, only by virtue of their tactile politics. However, much to my surprise, the latter considered homosexuality (especially the male version thereof) as some sort of spiritual qualification. Well, in that respect I was highly underqualified. Is that the reason why my spiritual practice didn't make the progress I was expecting?

Being very unaccustomed to this strangulation of spontaneity that I discovered in Brutland, I tried hard to find some trauma in the collective unconscious of the natives that would justify such a thing. It all seems to stem from the Victorian era:

> In late Victorian England, by contrast, and especially in the last quarter of the nineteenth century, we find a very different atmosphere—an atmosphere in which homosexual activities in the schools are now recognized, constantly suspected and regarded with horror. All associations between boys are seen as potentially vicious, and automatically so if the boys are from different age-groups. Friendship was seen as a mark of immorality and was therefore frowned on. In marked contrast to earlier Victorian England, in this later period spontaneous expressions of affection between males are regarded as taboo. We now have the growth of the stiff-upper-lip attitude which makes any personal emotion undesirable—an attitude eminently suited to the proconsuls of Empire being trained in the public schools.

—**Christie Davies**, *Permissive Britain*, p. 127

"Displays" of Lechery or the Arcane Art of Flirting

The author of the New York Times article, a certain Lena Williams, began it as follows: "By any definition, I am a flirt. I have been known to adjust men's ties when they're perfectly straight. To cup another's hand during an introductory handshake. To wink ever so slightly at alluring strangers across a crowded room, and to end conversations with the endearment 'sweetheart'".

The punctuation apart, how can she confess to being so ghastly—let alone to being proud of it! I would travel a million miles to get away from a person like that. Displays of lechery at the office Christmas party are much more acceptable than her kind of behaviour. They are at least honest and straightforward, and therefore much easier to deal with.

—*The Guardian*, 14/12/1996

They have got rid of the Christian God, and now feel obliged to cling all the more firmly to Christian morality: this is English consistency... In England, in response to every emancipation from theology one has to reassert one's position in a fear-inspiring manner as a moral fanatic.

—**Friedrich Nietzsche**, *Twilight of the Idols*: "Expeditions of an Untimely Man", 5

It is for this reason [sexual segregation] we can neither accept a compliment nor reject a pass, or at least not with the slightest grace. Also for this reason the pleasure of doing trivial things with the opposite sex, like hanging out or having lunch or shopping, is denied to us for ever. When Englishmen and women meet, it is always with an air of purpose—for work or courtship, by prior, formal arrangement.

—*Vogue*, January 1997, p. 89

This is the only country in Europe where young men think
if they don't drink eight pints on Friday night people will
call them a poof.

—*The Guardian*, 28/12/1996 (The year in review by Catherine Bennett)

The rolling English drunkard made the rolling
English road.
A reeling road, a rolling road, that rambles round
the shire.

—**G. K. Chesterton**, *The Rolling English Road.*

Macduff: What three things does drink especially pro-
voke?
Porter: Marry, sir, nose-painting, sleep, and urine.
Lechery, sir, it provokes, and unprovokes. It provokes
the desire, but it takes away the performance: therefore, much drink may be said to be an equivocator with
lechery: it makes him and it mars him; it sets him on,
and it takes him off; it persuades him, and disheartens
him; it makes him stand to and not stand to; in conclusion, equivocates him in a sleep, and giving him the lie,
leaves him.

—**William Shakespeare**, *Macbeth*

I shall attempt to guide the novice through the labyrinth of
native sexuality—and, specifically, through the sexuality characteristic of the male of the species and more aptly pertaining to
the sphere of that pre-coital overture known as *flirting*. It should
be noted that my conclusions have been reached after painstaking zoological observation in various contexts in which the
mating ritual is permitted. In most cases, my observations were
nurtured in venues like *pubs* and *clubs*. Let me make a fine distinction at this point, and introduce some special terminology,
as those inexperienced at the workings of the species might yet
have some unanswered questions.

Pubs is the general term applied to the natural habitat in which the great majority of the species exercises its social rituals regardless of age (anybody over eighteen), sex, social class, beliefs, etc. As a university guide for Incoming Erasmus Students says: "A good deal of English social life, especially for the young and unattached, centres on the pub".

Clubs is a more exclusive habitat in which mating patterns of the young and unattached achieve a higher level of intensity. However, in both these venues, the consumption of yeast extract is a *must*. It is the social ritual *par excellence*. Not just that, but it would be considered an insult to the male's virility to consume yeast extract in less than pint quantities. A *pint* is another culture-specific term which refers to the glass container of yeast extract, commonly known as *beer* in other species. So, if a native suggests that you should *go for a pint* he means to *go for a beer*.

A male would not dream of manifesting or expressing in any way whatsoever familiarity or interaction with the female of the species had he not beforehand consumed a minimum of five pints. Of course, this depends on the individual's idiosyncrasy and physical stamina. And indeed, a resistance to this substance is considered to be the *sine qua non* of manhood. Women are actually known to divorce men who have repeatedly proved to have a tolerance below five pints. (I've actually heard it in a pub: "No, I wouldn't go with a man who cannot take his pints"!)

To recapitulate, the possibility of expressing sexual behaviour begins with the milestone of the fifth pint. At this point the male becomes irritated, disquieted, frustrated, and myopic—as a miraculous metamorphosis takes place. And indeed, this far exceeds any other transformational phenomenon in the natural universe; it goes far beyond the metamorphosis of a larva into a butterfly.

What happens next? Well, the individual animal, from his prior state of *a priori penislessness*, metamorphoses into a huge, wobbling, pulsating phallus, preparing a massively imminent, womb-drenching explosion of penis extract. In such a state, the myopic animal will seize upon anything that moves and remotely resembles a female of the species. If he is lucky enough, the female will condescend and the flirting ritual will begin. During this time, of course, the consumption of liquid yeast extract continues, culminating in a total of seven, eight, or even nine pints. In such a state the male will follow the female to her nest in order for the procreation ritual to take place. But, as it so happens with most of these cases, due to an excessive consumption of yeast extract, the huge, wobbling, pulsating phallus will alchemically re-metamorphose into a tiny little piece of shit that would remain undetectable even under the scientific scrutiny of the world's most powerful microscope.

Funnily enough, at the end of a long night's "entertainment", the state of *a posteriori penislessness* (after the small "penisfulness" interval in-between) goes hand-in-hand with *pennylessness* which, to a certain degree, explains the financial shortcomings of students.

෨

> "So what is the true English sexual vice?", I asked.
> Julien became pompous, "Cuckoldry".
> "Not alcohol?", I asked sweetly.
> —**Maria Alvarez**, "Smack Habits", GQ, December 1996, p. 100

Native promiscuity (and native *drunken* debauchery) is the inevitable outcome of a censored, and consequently abstemious, attitude towards the art of flirting, ultimately linked to the general impoverished view of all things amorous. In other words, having been deprived of the possibility of playing the sweet game of flirtation, and of freely savouring the excitement of passionate emotional states, they attempt to compensate by means of *quantity* rather than than *quality*.

Inebriation is not an event that occurs with the intention of *jouissance*, transcendence, creativity, overflow of emotion, but is rather a monotonous reversion to an oblivious state of mind. In other words, it is not romantic inebriation in the vein of Keats ("Oh give me women, wine and snuff / 'Till I cry out 'Hold, enough!'") or Baudelaire ("Get drunk... with wine, with poetry, or with virtue, as you choose!") but the nauseous stupor of a suburban mouse drunk on the rather less exalted vintage found in sewers. (Actually, the best lager I tasted in England was Czechoslovakian: *Tatran*.)

And have you ever seen a mouse drunk on *amour, vertu* or *poésie?*

Sex is something that usually takes place in the heart of the "dark hours" (late at night and early in the morning), preferably under the *non compos mentis* excuse of being "drunk and disorderly". Deviation from this pattern, either in the form of male exhortations towards a day-time intercourse or as a non-pissed-out-of-your-head approach, signify outright lechery and are often thought to be the behavioural traits of culturally underprivileged individuals and foreigners.

I shall recount an event that took place whilst I was researching the one-night-stand phenomenon. I had been to the legendary Cavern, in Scouseland, the club where the Beatles used to play. I noticed one lady sitting next to someone of the same sex but rather older—she seemed old enough to be her mother or aunt. As the evening unfolded and the flirtation between us (in the shape of innuendo-imbued half-clandestine glances) increased, we finally found ourselves dancing together and chatting. At the end of the night I suggested that we go somewhere together, but she was reluctant: she was staying with her aunt, she had to return to the hotel. She said, "It would be nice *to shag your brains out,* but honestly there is no way I could make it tonight, you see my aunt wouldn't let me".

Her choice of metaphor conjured up an image morbid enough for the spookiest thriller. In fact, it brought me to the verge of nausea. And as if that were not enough, I even remembered something I had read by an English author by the name of Malcolm Muggeridge: "It has to be admitted that we English have sex on the brain, which is a very unsatisfactory place to have it", which had puzzled me then and didn't make things easier now. The image employed by this girl lent further credence to my suspicion that these people were keen on performing weird sadomasochistic rites that were not exactly my cup of tea. "*I would rather keep my brains in my skull during sex if you don't mind, thank you very much*", I thought, as I imagined my brains escaping my head and joining her astral brains somewhere above our bodies in the midst of sexual intercourse. I was so terrified by that image that I swore to abandon further fieldwork in identified public sex environments. "*How can you shag my brains out?*", I managed to murmur in consternation, only to recover from the shock a few years later when my grasp of idiomatic English had improved.

⁓

> Recreational drinking sometimes results directly from squalor, overwork and underpay, but sometimes also from the possession of funds without an accompanying tradition which ensures their constructive application.
>
> —**Brian Harrison**, *Drink and the Victorians*, p. 393

In other words, their "hedonistic" excesses are desperate reactions to the triple tyranny of deeply ingrained and culturally procured *anaphia* (inability to touch), *anhedonia* (inability to experience pleasure), and *aphilokalia* (inability to experience beauty). *Alexithymia* (emotional repression) comes as a natural corollary to all of these. Indeed, the natives' hedonistic excesses stand for the death throes of unlived pleasures and the false simulacra of convivialtity (which disintegrate with the "mo[u]rning after") that accompany that funeral procession which they euphemistically call *life*.

Look on the Bright Side of... Death

> This capacity to absorb the world and reforge it that has become one of our greatest strengths. In fact, I would suggest, perhaps our only strength.
>
> —**Nicholas Lezard**, "In Praise of British Women", *GQ*, 12/1996, p. 176

All things considered, one should not complain very much about how things are in Brutland, lest one undergo a Kafkaesque metamorphosis into a *whinging pommy*. With a bit of effort one can build a little heaven in hell's despair.

For a start, the dissolution of the family institution has come to mean that children over eighteen might have to pay rent for staying in the family nest (if the nucleus has not decided to downsize precisely in order to avoid such "house guests"); on the other hand, there is a liberal spirit which does not suppress the children's individuality and allows them to "do their own thing" and look as "deviant" as they wish.

Moreover, the apparent lack of generosity in social and family relations is balanced by widespread charitable activity—or is it that formalized giving makes the concept of giving more palatable?

Similarly, high praise must be bestowed upon its relatively generous social system, which compensates for the lack of generous family relationships; under its auspices you may be born, grow up, go on holidays, die, and get buried without ever having to work. Despite its many faults[1] it is still one of the best in the world. In the same vein the existence of *Family Planning Clinics* is a most altruistic bonus: many a pauper is now able to afford safe sex: these clinics individually dispense enough condoms to keep a harem's gestational level at zero for a whole season.

I would not do justice to Brutland if I failed to add that it has one of the best (and most expensive) postal systems in the world. Letters posted *first class* with the British Isles as their destination will arrive within a day—compare for example with Italy where the same service would take a week. And, speaking of Italy—the Italians have voted the *Jaguar* the best-designed car in the world. I have to admit that, although I'm not a car fan, I absolutely agree with them. One should also mention the *BBC*, the best television company in the world, *hackney carriages* (although Greeks find that they remind them of hearses), public libraries, tea-shops, foreign restaurants (thank God for that!), buskers and street-artists, and the countryside—when it's not raining or freezing cold, that is.

A number of other things bless this land with their gratuitous non-existence such as flies, bikers who use their bikes as penis extensions, excessive heat, rabies, dysentery and other exotic diseases.

And, last but not least (an expression the natives adore), I should mention the rare sense of humour, which although not a trademark of its denizens, can be found in a number of outstanding comedians and excellent sitcoms. Thus, we can say that humour in Brutland has a museum-like quality, since it is mostly experienced vicariously, through works of (usually) tele-

---

[1] One of the faults is that you can only qualify for unemployment allowance if you have a permanent address—thus those who need it more than anybody else, half a million homeless people, are left without any financial assistance at all.

vised art. However, when I watch an episode from *Only Fools and Horses*, *Steptoe & Son*, *Red Dwarf* or the *Black Adder* (to name but a few), I feel such a great gratitude for this nation that I could forgive them almost everything; if I was served a nice portion of *rhubarb crumble* with thick and creamy *custard*, that is.

Goodbye To All That

Your Englishman, confronted by something abnormal, will always pretend that it isn't there. If he can't pretend that, he will look through the object, or round it, or above it or below it, or in any direction except into it. If, however, you *force* him to look into it, he will at once pretend that he sees the object not for what it is but for something that he would like it to be.

—**James Agate**, *The Selective Ego*, "Ego 1" (ed. by Tim Beaumont, 1976), entry for 14/10/1932.

Perhaps the most intimate and exciting of all statements is to look deeply into the eyes of another.

—**Robert Hobson**, *Forms of Feeling*, p. 124

I saw the bag-lady again. Funny, I'd guessed she was there before actually seeing her by virtue of the intense smell that invaded my nostrils. "This is a familiar stench", I thought, and I was not mistaken in my assumption. She was there in the refectory, smoking her cigarette, completely out of context, utterly forlorn, like Alice in Studentland. She looked at me straight in the eye. For five years now, in Redbrick, nobody had ever honoured me so much. I almost felt *love*...

I left the refectory. The refectory with the coprophagous students (at times interspersed with coprophagous professors), the corpus linguisticians who specialized in the *corpus diplomaticus*, the waitresses with funny accents, the bored, middle-aged ladies at the till who would say *ta luv* and *tarrah luv*, the bag-lady...

Yeah, the stinking bag-lady.

Perhaps, the only thing of value.

Epitaph

This dissertation which constitutes an integral part of my degree in Creative Suffering is almost finished and will soon have to be submitted. In my case, the past is indeed a foreign country. However, I have a fear. I have a fear that it will be marked by an examiner that hasn't got the faintest idea about this kind of suffering. I only hope that not many marks will be deducted because of my footnoting. Sometimes it is rather erratic...

"Why have you written this book?", somebody may ask...

> After 6 months of doing nothing, Picasso has worked in a 6-week burst of outraged energy to complete a cubist canvas nearly 26 feet long filled with bedlam and terror that expresses the painter's horror at the brutality of modern warfare. When asked by the Germans the reason for which he produced this work he said: "it wasn't me who did this, it was *you*".

Now, you see, I am an older Spiros Doikas. I have lived through a lot and "a better and a wiser man I rose the morrow morn". Well, I don't like showing off, but now my full name—as you surely have noticed from the cover of this item—is *Spiros Doikas BA, MSc, KGB, Lav. Att.*, and I have all the qualifications that will enable me to come to grips with life, be happy, and, above all— *find success*.

"What are you?", people may ask. "An academic? A KGB spy? A Reichian radical? A new-age hippy? A psychedelic psychotherapist?". And I will grin dismissively, "Nought o' the sort. Just an under-privileged, over-qualified Lavatory Attendant, and if you don't believe it come to see me at Euston where I work, mate, and I'll tell you stories... I'll tell you the story of a couple who had it here, *big time*, here man, in the loos... and if you don't believe me, I'll tell you this, *I had to call the fire service to clean up the spunk*... but, hey, soft lad, don't forget to bring your 20p. with you... and some serviettes or something... I just hate it when people try to make an identified public sex environment out of my lavatory..."

E quindi uscimmo a riveder le stelle...

Epilogue

Brutish:
1. Of or pertaining to the brutes, or lower animals, as opposed to man
2. Pertaining to, resembling or characteristic of the brutes
3. Rough, rude, savage, brutal
4. Brute
5. obs. form of British

—**Oxford English Dictionary**, 1988 edition

Who the first inhabitants of Britain were, whether natives or immigrants, remains obscure; one must remember we are dealing with barbarians.

—**Tacitus**, *Agricola*, sct. 11

He is a barbarian, and thinks that the customs of his tribe and island are the laws of nature.

—**George Bernard Shaw**, *Caesar and Cleopatra*, act 2:
Caesar speaking of Britannus, his secretary, "an islander from the western end of the world, a day's voyage from Gaul".

*T*he obvious conclusion that can be adduced from the preceding remarks is that *Englishness* is a rather grave genetic defect and a major behavioural dysfunction of personality; in other words, something to be got over as soon as possible for the sake of the individual's sanity and general well-being. With this end in mind, my modest proposal is that special boarding schools be built abroad, financed by Her Majesty's Government, whose exclusive aim would be to propound and skilfully impart a curriculum of *De-Anglification* (leading to the concomitant state of *De-Uglification*) to the totality of the afflicted population. Naturally, I realise the grandiose proportions of this undertaking; nevertheless, I consider it the most important undertaking ever if we want our tribe to survive and achieve an H.Q. (Happiness Quotient) slightly above the suicidal state and even, if I am not being too optimistic, transform its onanistic *joie de ivre*[2] into *joie de vivre*.

I consider myself a rarely seen philanthropist (perhaps worthy of an OBE, a CBE, or, who knows, even a knighthood), an individual who, with utmost sympathy for their chequered past, altruistically envisages an *Englishless* future for the English people, or, should I say, a *detribalized future* for the *English nation*. As perhaps the only true prophet of *Englishlessness*, I am willing to hazard the fragile equilibrium of my own *Englishness-free psyche* by urging them to rid themselves of their *selective serotonin re-uptake inhibitors* and specialize in *getting a life*. So...

> Enough of solitary vice
> Better carve yourself a slice
> Of life, for as the poet said,
> There's fuck-all fucking when you're dead.

> —John Whitworth

---

[2] "Joie de ivre" (joy of drunkenness) is a pun ("ivre" means "drunk" in French) with "joie de vivre" (joy of living).

Bibliography

ANTHROPOLOGY

Marshall, Jack and Drysdale, Russell, *Journey among Men*, 1962,

Paz, Octavio, *The Labyrinth of Solitude*, Penguin, London, 1985

Philips, Caryl, *The European Tribe*, Faber, London/Boston, 1987

Silentiarius, Paulus, *Onanistan— an anthropological guide*, Intergalactic publications, The Big Crater, Mars, Star date 2309

BRITAIN AND THE BRITISH

Anonymous, *Onania; or, the Heinous Sin of Self-Pollution, and All its Frightful Consequences*, Thomas Crouch, London, 1723

Aperson, G.L., *English Proverbs and proverbial phrases*, London, J.M. Dent and Sons Ltd., 1929

Appleyard, B., *The Essential Anatomy of Britain*, Hodder & Stoughton, 1992

Boucé, Paul-Gabriel (ed), *Sexuality in eighteenth-century Britain*, Manchester UP, 1982, Manchester.

Brown, Isaac Baker, *On the Curability of Certain Forms of Insanity, Epilepsy, Catalepsy, and Hysteria in Females*, Cox and Wyman, 1866

Browne, Sir Thomas, *Religio Medici*

Bryson, Bill, *Notes from a small island*, Doubleday, London, 1995

Cheyne, George, *The English Malady; or, A Treatise of Nervous Diseases of all Kinds, with the Author's Own Case* (1733)

Clarke, Cas, *Grub on a Grant*, Columbus Books, London, 1986

Costello, Peter, *The Dublin Literary Pub Crawl*, Dublin, A & A Farmar, 1996

Davies, Christie, *Permissive Britain*, Pitman Publishing, London, 1975

Defoe, Daniel, *The True-Born Englishman*.

Ferris, Paul, *Sex and the British, A twentieth century history*, Michael Joseph, London, 1993

Grosvenor, Peter & McMillan, James, *The British Genius*, Coronet Books, London, 1974

Hoch, Paul & Schoenbach, Vic, *LSE: The Natives are Restless—A Report on Student Power in Action*,

Sheed and Ward, London and Sydney, 1969

Hoggart, Richard, *The Uses of Literacy*, Penguin, Harmondsworth, Middlesex, 1959

Hoggart, Richard, *The Way We Live Now*, Pimlico, London, 1995

Leavis, F. R., *English Literature in our time and the University*, CUP, Cambridge, 1969

MacFarlane, Alan, *The Origins of English Individualism: The Family, Property and Social Transition*, Blackwell, December 1978

Mascuch, Michael, *Origins of the Individualist Self : Autobiography and Self-Identity in England, 1591-1791*, Stanford University Press / January 1997

Mennel, Stephen, *All Manners Of Food*, Blackwel, 1985

Miall, Antony, *Xenophobe's guide to the English*, Ravette Publishing, West Sussex, 1993

Mikes, George, *How to be a Brit*, Penguin, England, 1984

Mikes, George, *How to be an Alien*, Penguin, England, 1966

Morris, C., *The Origins of English Individualism*, Blackwell, Oxford, 1987

Orwell, George, "The English People". 1944; repr. in *The Collected Essays, Journalism and Letters of George Orwell*, vol. 3, ed. by Sonia Orwell & Ian Angus, 1968)

Osmond, John, *The Divided Kingdom*, Constable, London, 1988

Robertson, John, *Morrissey In His Own Words*, Omnibus Press, London, NY, Sydney, 1988

Room, Adrian, *The A to Z of British Life*, OUP, 1990

Santayana, George, *Soliloquies in England*

Shah, Idries, *Darkest England*, Octagon Press, London, 1987

Shah, Idries, *The Natives Are Restless*, Octagon Press, London, 1988

DIARIES

Trotsky, Leon, *Diary in Exile*, 1959

Silentiarius, Paulus, *The Onanistan Diaries* (unpublished)

DRAMA/CINEMA

Craig, W. J. (ed), The Complete Works of William Shakespeare, Magpie Books, London, 1992

George Bernard Shaw, *Heartbreak House*

Oscar Wilde, *A Woman of no Importance*

Oscar Wilde, *The Importance of Being Earnest*

Oscar Wilde, *The Picture of Dorian Gray*

Simon Beaufoy, *The Full Monty*, ScreenPress Books, England, 1997

Terence Rattigan, *The Collected*

Plays, (Vol IV), *In Praise of Love*, Hamish Hamilton, London, 1978

FICTION

Amis, Kingsley, *Lucky Jim*, London, Victor Gollancz Ltd, 1965

Austen, Jane, *Emma*, Wordsworth Classics, Great Britain, 1994

Austen, Jane, *Northhanger Abbey*, Worsworth Classics, Great Britain, 1993

Bradbury, Malcolm (ed), *Modern British Short Stories*, Penguin, England, 1988

Burnett, Frances Hodgson, *The Secret Garden*, Penguin, England, 1995

Ishiguro, Kazuo, *The Remains of The Day*, Faber & Faber, London, 1989

Lodge, David, *Changing Places*, Penguin, Great Britain, 1978

Magee, Bryan, *Facing Death*, William Kimber, London, 1977

Miller, Henry, *The Colossus of Maroussi*, Penguin, 1950

Solzhenitsyn, Alexander, *Cancer Ward*, Penguin, Harmondsworth, Middlesex, 1968

Swift, Jonathan, *Gulliver's Travels*, Wordsworth Classics, Herfordshire, 1992

Vonnegut, Kurt, *Breakfast of Champions*, Jonathan Cape Ltd, London, 1973

Wilde, Oscar, *The Picture of Dorian Gray*

Wilde, Oscar, *An Ideal Husband*

Wimmer, Kurt, *Equilibrium* (film), 2002

HUMOUR

Cagney, Peter, *The Book of Wit and Humour*, Thorsons, 1976

Cole, William & Philips, Louis, *Sex: "The most fun you can have without laughing"*, Castle Books, USA, 1997

Metclaf, Fred, *Penguin Dictionary of Humorous Quotations*, Harmondsworth, Middlesex, England, 1986

Sherrin, Ned, *The Oxford Dictionary of Humorous Quotations*, OUP, Oxford, 1995

MAGAZINES

FHM

GQ

Grip (UMIST University student's magazine)

Lakeside magazine (Swiss magazine written in English)

More!

Vogue

NEWSPAPERS

The Athens News

The Church of England Newspaper

The Courts Homewatch (a Manchester Newsletter about

a Hulme Council Residential
Area)

The Daily Star

The Daily Telegraph

The Express

The Financial Times

The Guardian

The Independent

The Independent on Sunday

The Irish Sunday Independent

The Manchester Evening News

The Manchester Metro News

The Observer

The Sunday Telegraph

The Sunday Times

The Times

The Yorkshire Post

PHILOSOPHY

Artaud, Antonin, *Letter to the Chancellors of the European Universities* (published in *Collected Works*, vol. 1, pt. 2, 1956; tr. 1968).

Hesse, Herman, *Aforismi*, Tascabili Edizioni Newton, Italy, 1994

Levy, Oscar (ed), *The complete Nietzsche, Ecce Homo, Why I am so clever*—Vol XVII, Gordon Press, New York, 1974

Nietzsche, Friedrich, *Daybreak*, Translated by R.J. Hollingdale, CUP, Cambridge, 1982

Nietzsche, Friedrich, *Twilight of the Idols/The Anti-Christ*, Penguin, England, 1968

Racionero, Luis, *Las Filosofias Del Underground*, Editorial Anagrama, Madrid, 1977

Rand, Ayn, *The Romantic Manifesto*, Signet, New York, 1975

POETRY

Byron, Lord, *Collected Poems*

Eliot, T.S., *Complete poems*

Larkin, Philip, *Collected Poems*, Marvell Press, 1988

McGough, Roger, *After the merrymaking*, Jonathan Cape, London, 1971

Rochester, Earl of, *Selected Poetry*

PSYCHOLOGY/ SOCIOLOGY

Buber, Martin, *I and Thou*, T. & T. Clarke, Edinburg, 1937

Foucault, Michel, *Discipline and Punish*, Allen Lane, London, 1975

Freud, Sigmund, *Civilization, Society and Religion*, Vol. 12, Penguin, London, 1985

Fromm, Erich, *The Sane Society*, Routledge & Kegan Paul, London, 1956

Goleman, Daniel, *Emotional Intelligence*, Bloomsbury Publishing, Great Britain, 1996

Hobson, Robert, *Forms of Feeling, The Heart of Psychotherapy*, London, Tavistock, 1985

Laplanche, J. & Pontalis, B., *The Language of Psychoanalysis*, Karnac and the Institute of Psychoanalysis, 1988

Pasolini, Pier Paolo, *Droga e Cultura, Il Caos*, Editori Riuniti, Roma, 1979

Reich, Wilhelm, *The Function of the Orgasm*, Farrar, Straus and Girou, 1986

Sifneos, Peter, *Affect, Emotional Conflict and Deficit: An Overview*, in *Psychotherapy and Psychosomatics*, 56, p. 116-22

Steinem, Gloria, *The Myth of Masculine Mystique*

Szasz, Thomas, *The Second Sin*, Social Relations, 1973

Vries, Jan de, *Stress and Nervous Disorders*, Mainstream Publishing, Great Britain, 1985

REFERENCE

Collins English Dictionary, Millenium Edition, Harper Collins Publishers, 1988,

Partridge, Eric, *A dictionary of slang and unconventional English*, Routledge & Kegan Paul, London, 1984

Lewin, Esther & Albert, *The Wordsworth Thesaurus of Slang*, Herfordshire, Glasgow, 1995

Green, Jonathon, *The Slang Thesaurus*, Penguin Books, England, 1988

Oxford English Dictionary, 1988

Wikipedia

STUDENT PROSPECTUSES

Manchester "Sub Student Handbook", SUBlime Publications, 1993-4

University of Manchester, *A guide for Incoming Erasmus Students*, June 1994 edition

SPIRITUALITY

Kornfield, Jack, *A Path with Heart, A Guide Through the Perils and Promises of Spiritual Life*, Bantam Books, New York, 1993

Gibran, Khalil, *Prophet, Madman, Wanderer*, Penguin 60's, Penguin, London, 1995

Gibran, Khalil, *Sand and Foam*

Sangharakshita, *Vision and Transformation*, Windhorse Publications, Birmingham, 1990

Suzuki, Shunryu, *Zen Mind, Beginner's Mind*, Weatherhill, New York, 1991

Rinpoche, Sogyal, *The Tibetan Book of Living and Dying*, Rupa & Co, 1993

Index

Made in the USA
Charleston, SC
13 April 2013